MESSENGERS OF
ENCOURAGEMENT

DAVID HAGSTROM

Paperback ISBN: 978-1-945587-62-7
Library of Congress Control Number: 2021907391
1. Self-help; 2. Memoir; 3. Encouragement; 4. Essay

Book editing and design: Dancing Moon Press
Cover photo: Scott Thompson, Bristol, Wisconsin
Author photo: Karen Noordhoff, Portland, Oregon
Manufactured in the United States of America

Dancing Moon Press
Bend, Oregon
dancingmoonpress.com

Grateful acknowledgement is hereby tendered to the copyright
holders for permission to reprint the following items:
The stories "My Thank to the Dean" and "The Blue Bicycle
Summer," as well as Daniel H. Kim's poem "Calling" are
republished with permission of John Wiley & Sons Inc. from *From
Outrageous To Inspired: How To Build a Community of Leaders in Our
Schools* by David Hagstrom, 2003; permission conveyed through
Copyright Clearance Center, Inc. Daniel H. Kim's poem is also
used with permission of the author, Founding Trustee, Society for
Organizational Learning.

Virginia Satir, "Greatest Gift" is used with permission of the
Virginia Satir Global Network, Wendell, North Carolina, www.
satirglobal.org. All rights reserved.

William Stafford, "You Reading This, Be Ready" and "The Way
It Is" are from *Ask Me: 100 Essential Poems*. Copyright © 1977,
1980, 1998 by William Stafford and the Estate of William Stafford.
Reprinted with the permission of The Permissions Company,
LLC on behalf of Graywolf Press, Minneapolis, Minnesota, www.
greywolfpress.org.

For Karen
My Story Lady

CONTENTS

FOREWORD

Here's the most important thing you need to know about this book, in addition to the fact that it's very well-written. The author, a beautiful man I've known for twenty years, does more than "walk his talk." He embodies the book's title in every fiber of his being. Anyone who's known David Hagstrom during the eighty-five years he's graced the earth will testify that, to the core, *he* is a messenger of encouragement for all who cross his path.

David's book is a beautiful collection of vivid and engaging stories about messengers who've shown up in his life to help him take next steps in good and not-so-good times. As you read them, you'll be doing far more than learning about David's journey— you'll be seeing your own journey more clearly as David opens your eyes to messengers who've crossed your path with blessings you may have missed. You'll also receive gentle guidance, as I have, about how to show up as a messenger of encouragement to others.

Talking about these stories is no substitute for the stories themselves. So without giving the plot away, I want to offer a taste of what's inside this lovely book by recapping a couple of David's tales (which still need to be read in full in order to appreciate them fully).

The first story is about David at age 12. He describes himself as "a very quiet fellow" back then. That's a quality that parents of pre-teens might be grateful for, but one that can put a boy on the margins among his gregarious age-mates.

David was blessed with an understanding mother, who said,

"David is just finding his voice, and in the meantime, he is listening with great care." That's a strong message of encouragement. But who among us took our parents' affirmations seriously when we were afflicted with the condition called growing up? Those of us with good parents found it easy to discount such messages by thinking, "That's just the kind of thing a mother would say."

On a winter camping trip with his scout troop, David took refuge in a corner of a tent large enough for the whole troop, hoping to get some sleep. But the other scouts wanted to talk, and so they did, on into the night. Every now and then, a friend of David's would call out, "David, say a word," to which David would respond, "A word." Eventually, realizing that his friend was trying to embarrass him, David changed his reply to "listening."

The next morning, as David and the scoutmaster built a fire to cook breakfast while the troop slept, the scoutmaster became a messenger of encouragement:

> I heard the word you spoke last night: listening. The day will come when you grow into that word even more deeply. Those around you will see you coming and say to themselves, "Good, David is on his way." You probably won't say many words, but everyone will know a careful listener is present, and be glad.

The scoutmaster let David know that he saw and heard him, and in doing so, he encouraged David to realize he was accepted just as he was.

I am one of many who is able to say that the scoutmaster got it exactly right.

Fast forward to 1982. David was 47 years old when an MRI revealed that he had a brain tumor "the size of a large tangerine." Repair required a sixteen-hour surgery plus twenty-five days in the hospital, from which David emerged marked in ways that remain with him to this day.

A nurse named Jill drew the happy duty of caring for David during his nights in recovery. She always took time to talk, often asking David life-giving questions. One night, she asked him, "What song do you deeply love?" David answered, "Without a

Song." The following night Jill brought in a portable device and played Willie Nelson's cover, which brought tears to both their eyes.

The next week, having recalled that David had said, "Music taps into my heart"—and knowing that David was struggling with hearing loss—Jill said, "So now you'll be our Heart Man. You will listen to your favorite songs and those of many others. You'll listen with your heart, and you'll hear their soul songs."

It took him time, but eventually David came to understand what Jill meant:

> Later, the skill I learned through speech and hearing rehabilitation helped me function again in the world of hearing people, but I found that without the usual physical process to help me hear, I began to turn more and more to listening in other ways. My ears have considerable difficulty perceiving sounds these days; however, my heart has become a deeper, more trustworthy source of hearing. There's a song strong in my soul. I hear my song—and other people's too. I listen with my heart.

I find two messengers of encouragement in this story: Jill with her gifts of discernment and blessing, and David with his capacity to find the ability on the other side of disability.

One more thing: There is no way for me to summarize, or even characterize, the last section of this book, which David titled "Last Words." All I can say is, "Read it—you'll be glad you did."

David, on behalf of your readers and your many friends, thank you for your deep listening and words of encouragement, for so generously sharing your heart. The world is a better place because of you and your gifts, and we who would be messengers of encouragement are grateful.

—Parker J. Palmer, author of *On the Brink of Everything, Let Your Life Speak, The Courage to Teach* and *Healing the Heart of Democracy*

WELCOME

I'm grateful you've found your way here. I hope you'll enjoy my stories about the power of encouragement. I hope you'll begin remembering your own most meaningful moments of being encouraged or offering encouragement.

My keen interest in encouragement probably had one of its origins in my childhood, on the school playground. Almost always the last one chosen for softball games, I felt tormented incessantly. "Oh, no! Strikeout David. Not again!" I was utterly discouraged until our well-loved physical education teacher walked me the four blocks home one afternoon, asking about my hobbies and interests along the way. When we arrived at my front porch, he proposed, "Let's meet on the playground each morning next week before school begins. We'll have some batting practice. I'll share with you some snazzy tricks to help you bat better."

Remembering and deliberating about encouragement has caused me to realize that encouragement can be at the same time simple and profound. On the one hand, there's the simple verbal form: "May your day go well, my friend." There is the physical form: "Let me give you a hand with that lifting. The two of us will make the task much easier." On the other hand, conveying to someone that you deeply believe in them might well be the ultimate form of encouragement.

For example, when I was a senior in high school, I wanted to become a cabinetmaker; I admired family members who worked with wood as their livelihood. Much to my surprise, my guidance counselor called me into his office, saying, "David, why don't you consider going to college? I know you could handle it." I recount this story in "My Thank You to the Dean." Later as an experienced educator I was a candidate for the position of Commissioner of Education in Alaska and felt most grateful to receive letters of recommendation from teachers I knew who also enthusiastically stated their beliefs in my capacities.

There are those times when encouraging can go awry. Encouraging with the intent to "fix" a person can cause irritation and resentment. Advising as a form of encouragement has never worked for me. I've learned over the years that each of us has an inner voice we rely on for knowing what's right and what's wrong for us. It just doesn't work to try to correct and direct, when people have their own sense of what's right for themselves.

This book is a collection of stories about encouragement. Maybe you'll find yourself in my stories, too. I've always been entranced with the words of Frederick Buechner in his memoir, *Telling Secrets*:

> My story is important not because it is mine, God knows, but because if I tell it anything like right, the chances are you will recognize that in many ways it is also yours. Maybe nothing is more important than that we keep track, you and I, of these stories of who we are and where we have come from and the people we have met along the way because...to lose track of our stories is to be profoundly impoverished not only humanly but also spiritually.

I've written these stories over the years at my desk in what my wife and I call The Writing House. It's an exquisitely tiny, separate building that sits at the edge of the forest, the high desert, and the mountains near our cabin in central Oregon. It is a good place to remember who I am, to take stock, and to write about what I have learned in life.

I'm not sure how it is for other writers, but for me, being able to return to the same, familiar, and customary quiet place, day after day, inspires my sense of creativity. I need a place devoid of distractions. I need a comfortable space that allows me to settle into myself. For me to be able to concentrate, and carefully focus on those ideas that are ready to reveal themselves, I must find myself in a safe, peaceful haven. I can't just drop everything wherever I may be and begin to play with words. Rather, I return to The Writing House.

My early morning writing routine begins by placing my journal in my lap and awaiting whatever my pen has to offer, which is often a meager mishmash or modest in scope or insight. On rare occasion, I strike it rich and my pages reveal promising possibilities for the day's writing. Years ago, I realized that I write to learn what I know. Often, it takes numerous days working with my journal before I place my computer on the desk and begin playing with words in story form. I've also learned over the years that as I sort through joys, challenges, and confusing life events in my journal and stories, I end up in places where I've felt encouragement and gratitude for that encouragement.

Here, I share stories of encouragement throughout my life. As you read, you'll find that encouragement takes many different forms. We can simply *recognize* another person. We can call them by their name, acknowledging that they are truly known. We can take an appropriate *action*, accentuating the fact that encouragement is more than a feeling; it requires doing something. We can deeply, nonjudgmentally, *listen* to others. We can *affirm* the other, appreciating their unique gifts and talents. We can *ask open and honest questions*. Asking just the right question is a genuine gift. We can *offer* a very specific idea, in terms of a possibility. And finally, we can engage others in a process of *truth-telling*. Without being hurtful, we can offer what the other person might have missed.

I recount episodes of my being encouraged, such as my scoutmaster's life-giving affirmation and my most recent medical challenge. I also offer accounts about times I've witnessed others encouraging someone. There's the story of a father encouraging his son on the ice rink and a physician who practices "slow medicine." Finally, I write about those times I've tried to encourage. I relate my efforts as a school principal in "The Blue Bicycle Summer" and "Walking Them Home." Three angles on the same theme: encouragement.

W.S. Merwin, a Pulitzer Prize winner and former U.S. poet laureate, reminds us "I have only what I remember." Through my remembering, I find that rather easily now at age 85, I see myself more clearly. I'm accepting that I am who I am, and in the fundamentals of my identity, there's not as much room for change these days. That's just fine with me. I'm also not so focused on minutia, but am trying to keep my eye and heart centered on what's most important. I find myself to be quite content with my dedicated exploration of encouragement.

I'm writing in the hope that we might be, in some profound and unfathomable way, in a conversation about our experiences with encouragement. It can be easy to reflexively complain or find fault; it can be more difficult to encourage, to reassure. But together, we can explore the many ways of meaningfully caring for one another. I'm inviting you to join me as we create an ever-growing collection of stories about encouragement. It's a form of loving one another that is tolerable to almost everyone, can be learned by almost everyone, and is needed by every one of us. May we learn and practice together how to encourage more completely and more compassionately. May we become messengers of encouragement in a world that's yearning for greater personal and interpersonal understanding and well-being.

I believe
The greatest gift
I can conceive of having
from anyone
is
to be seen by them,
heard by them,
to be understood
and
touched by them.
The greatest gift
I can give
is
to see, hear, understand
and to touch
another person.
When this is done
I feel
contact has been made.

—Virginia Satir

CHILDHOOD YEARS

David, Say a Word

The Story Lady

David, Say a Word

A stern scoutmaster acknowledges and values who I really am.

When I was about 12 years old, my life was almost totally given over to Boy Scout interests. Our scoutmaster, Harold White, believed the way to transform boys into young men was through what he called "hardship activities." So the brave lads of Scout Troop 22 went on challenging campouts at least once a month throughout the entire year, even in the midst of the bleak winter of the American Midwest.

Outside of my own home, I was very much a quiet fellow in those days. (I still think of myself as not very talkative.) Except when I was playing basketball or baseball, I spoke only when spoken to or asked a question. Yes, I was that silent. I think then, as now, I enjoyed listening more than speaking. My mother said, "David is just finding his voice, and in the meantime, he is listening with great care. The day will come when he'll have a very strong voice, an encouraging voice."

One cold January night, fourteen Troop 22 scouts camped by a frozen river where the snow was two feet deep. We cozied ourselves inside sleeping bags spread across the floor of an enormous khaki-colored army surplus tent. I found myself in a somewhat isolated far corner and prepared for sleep. But sleep was not to be the order of the evening for me. My tent mates wanted to talk. And talk and talk. And talk some more. The chatter (about girls, hot rod cars, and teachers' dirty looks—in that order) went on for more than an hour. Every fifteen minutes or so, a scout friend would call over to my corner, "David, say a word." When first asked, I called back, "A word." There were chuckles all around. So, when asked a second and a third time,

I replied in the same way, "A word." I began to feel this scout friend was simply trying to be clever, while embarrassing me, so I changed my response to, "Listening."

The bantering continued until Scoutmaster White, who I'm sure actually took all this in with a big smile, declared sternly, "That's it, boys! All words will now cease! It'll be quiet time throughout the night. And when you awake, let every word spoken be very considerate and kind, and I hope you'll listen better to each other."

Like always, I was the first one up the next morning and helped Mr. White build the fire and get the pancakes going on the griddle. He whispered, "I heard the word you spoke last night: listening. The day will come when you grow into that word even more deeply. Those around you will see you coming and say to themselves, 'Good, David is on his way.' You probably won't say many words, but everyone will know a careful listener is present, and be glad." As just the two of us huddled around the campfire, I knew my scoutmaster was in my corner. He let me know that he saw and heard me and in doing so, he encouraged me to realize I was accepted just as I was.

Over the years, I believe I have grown into that person he named and appreciated.

The Story Lady

She opens worlds of possibility for me as a child and as an elder.

It was a quarter past one that Thursday afternoon, and I was eager with anticipation. In just fifteen minutes, all the other fourth graders and I would make the short trek across the street to be with The Story Lady. Sure enough, at the appointed time we walked out of our second-floor classroom at Whittier School in my hometown of Oak Park, Illinois, proceeded to the corner of Mapleton and Augusta, where the portable stoplight was attended by Officer Heap during school hours. We crossed the intersection and in three minutes we arrived at the Dole Branch Library.

The librarian, Miss Carolyn, told us that we had twenty minutes to turn in books and select new ones. "And remember," she said, "you all need to be in the south room at exactly two o'clock." We all knew what that meant: The Story Lady would soon be here. For me, and I think for most of my fellow students, being read to by The Story Lady was the highlight of the week, the best part of fourth grade.

As far as I knew at the time, the woman who read us stories each week had no other name. She was simply The Story Lady and I loved her. She was wise and adventurous; she took us to faraway places. And she had the most versatile voice. She could talk like a woman, or a man, or a girl, or a boy. She could even talk like an alligator! With those animated voices, she encouraged me to listen very carefully. She drew me into her realm and stories.

The Story Lady introduced me to so many brilliant people and carried me away to so many fascinating places. Once I traveled to Greenland through her reading and another time, I imagined being a part of the building of the transcontinental railroad.

One of my favorite stories from that year, Paul Gallico's *The Snow Goose*, captivated me. This story, set in World War II, centers on the friendship between an artist living with a disability in a lighthouse and a young child. The relationship begins with the wounding of a migrating snow goose and culminates in the artist's heroism in saving hundreds of civilians in the Battle of Dunkirk. Looking back on the story as an adult, I understand that it not only related to my life, but also took me beyond the boundaries of my life. For one thing, when The Story Lady read us the book, WWII was still raging and I was well aware that a neighbor with whom I'd been a pen pal had died in service. I also related to the child who was about my same age. I'd earlier become engrossed by lighthouses, an interest I carry even today. Yet the snow goose seemed unknown and mysterious to me. The story helped expand my understanding of what it meant to live with a disability as severe as the artist's and that a person with such a disability could be a hero. Other books that intrigued me were the fabulous adventure *Paddle-to-the-Sea* by Holling Clancy Holling and the enthralling *The Little Town on the Prairie* by Laura Ingalls Wilder, the first being a story based in geography and the second, an historical memoir. (Interestingly, I later became a teacher of history and geography.)

All these stories, chosen and read by The Story Lady, opened and enlarged my world. They inspired, motivated and encouraged me. She cultivated my wanderlust: I could travel to Greenland one day! She awakened my curiosity: How did people manage to live on the prairie in the 1880s? She helped me imagine how to relate to others different from myself: I could be a friend of a person with a disability, none of whom I was aware of knowing at that time. Most importantly, she nurtured my envisioning the world as full of possibilities of which I'd been unaware: I could help build a railroad; I could be a lighthouse keeper; I could work the land, being a gardener or farmer. In the process, she fostered my faith in my own potential: I could set my sights high. I was intrigued with how much folks did with what they had and I could do the same.

When I turned 75, The Story Lady appeared once again through the soothing voice of my wife, Karen. Like the original Story Lady, she is wise and adventurous. She began to read mystery stories to me, not in the mid-afternoon, but at nine o'clock in the evening as we prepared for sleep. For example, the Bruno, Chief of Police mystery series recounts the exploits of Benoit Courrèges, a policeman in a small French village where the rituals of the café still rule. She's read me a dozen of those books and I've been transported to the Dordogne River valley. Next, she read me the thirteen Louise Penny stories about the emotionally complex homicide detective Armand Gamache and his circle of friends and colleagues in the Quebeçois town of Three Pines. Over the past decade, The Story Lady has re-emerged and read hundreds of stories to me, by which I'm both energized and comforted and which, eventually, lull me to sleep.

I can relate to the French stories because they are set in villages such as those my wife and I have visited. I can relate to Armand Gamache in that relationships are all important to him, as they are to me. These days, just as when I was only eight years old, my wanderlust and motivation are activated through these stories. Come hell or high water, I'm going back to France! I'm encouraged to imagine such a possibility that at my present age might seem unimaginable. Through these stories and characters I'm transported out of my everyday concerns, issues, or problems into a world of possibility.

I'll never again hear The Story Lady from so many years ago, but The Story Lady of today is fortunately forever near and dear. What a fortunate fellow I am, having been read to as a child, and now again, as an elder. Over my lifetime, I've been encouraged by each Story Lady to dream big.

COLLEGE/UNIVERSITY

My Thank You to the Dean

The Truth-Telling Hour

You Call My Name

"Calling"

My Thank You to the Dean

"Making a difference" changes everything for me.

For all my work life, I've wanted to "make a difference." Almost seventy years ago, I received a gift that just might explain why.

I was a senior in a Chicago area high school, planning a school-to-work transition that involved getting a job in the building trades, perhaps as a cabinetmaker. Many members of my family were carpenters and painters, and I was planning to join them in some way. I wanted to work with my hands.

That is until what was called at the time the Dean of Senior Boys—basically my guidance counselor, Mr. Fritzmeier—surprised me with, "What are your plans for college, David?" Given that my dad had been out of work during the Depression, and henceforth my family practiced frugality, I suppose I'd assumed college couldn't be a part of my future. Nor did I see myself as much of an academic student. So, sort of stunned, I explained, "I'm not going to college. No one in our family has ever gone to college, we don't have much money at home, and I'm really looking forward to going into carpentry work." The dean, studying me, declared, "We'll see. Meet me in my office tomorrow, same time. Understand?"

I assured him, "Yes, tomorrow, same time."

The next day, the dean asked, "David, anything planned this weekend?"

Trying to recall any arranged "hot dates" or scheduled basketball "alley games," I realized nothing was scheduled.

"No big plans," I answered.

"Good," he said with a smile. "Be here on Friday at one o'clock, bag packed for the weekend. Don't worry about anything, just know that the two days you'll be away will be life-changing."

As the dean drove me downtown to Chicago's Rock Island railway station, he informed me, "You're traveling to Grinnell College in Iowa, and when you get there, someone will meet you. Here are your tickets. As the miles go by, enjoy the adventure of it all, knowing I believe in you. And one more thing. Be prepared to enthusiastically say, 'Yes, of course.'"

On my arrival at the Grinnell train station, I was greeted by a student and taken to a dorm for a rather unsettled "settling in." I wondered, what's going on? For the next day and a half, I sat in on classes, went to a dance, and talked with (what seemed at the time) the entire college community. Upon leaving the college on Sunday, I heard these words from one of the admissions staff: "We want you at Grinnell, David. All of your college expenses have been arranged for, and you'll work as our night switchboard operator. So, what do you say?"

As Mr. Fritzmeier had directed, I offered my enthusiastic, "Yes, of course."

Years later, I learned that the dean paid for that train trip with his own money and all but "sponsored" my stay at Grinnell. In a later conversation with him about all this, he revealed, "Your Grinnell gift was simply about my wanting to make a difference in the life of at least one person. By way of thanks, simply promise me you'll try to do the same, knowing all the while you may never know for sure that you've made that difference. Just keep on trying and watch for your chances with each new day." I'd guess and want to honor the likelihood that my parents also offered whatever they could in the way of some bit of financial support, yet it remains a mystery to me whether and how that happened and whether my mother and Mr. Fritzmeier may have developed some plan between them.

I did promise what Mr. Fritzmeier asked: trying, in essence, to encourage a positive prospect for those I meet in life. And, not knowing for sure whether I've yet made that difference, I continue to "watch for my chances." It's my thank you to the dean.

The Truth-Telling Hour

My academic advisor encourages me with a gift and a promise.

"Dave, my most significant learnings in life, the events that have made the most positive difference in my life, have all come as a result of failures." My academic advisor passed along these surprising words to me, as I questioned why I'd received a grade of D on my mid-term exam.

My professor, John Burma, greeted me with a broad smile as I arrived at his office, and this invitation: "I know why you're here. Thanks for coming to see me. Let's take a walk. I have a gift and a promise to present to you." We proceeded down the hall and entered a completely empty auditorium. In the balcony of that auditorium, as we sat side by side, Dr. Burma shared some personal incidents of difficulty, the traumas that had become, as he put it, "terra firma for every future success." In a whisper, he admitted, "Dave, I've learned practically nothing from my successes. All of the progress that has come to me has come from incidents like," and here he paused, "getting a D on a sociology exam."

Truthfully, my advisor's stories of failure didn't offer much comfort during that time of anguish. I was devastated. I thought that I would soon be Grinnell College history. Was Dr. Burma just giving me a way out, an invitation to move on to whatever was next?

As it turned out, John Burma's stories of failure weren't a way out; they were a way in, a way into learning about myself and learning how to learn. Over time, I've discovered for myself the truthfulness of his message. For instance, when I lost out on the Alaska Commission of Education position, I learned that I should watch out for my ego as a driver of my vocation. That mid-term D and the conversation with Dr. Burma led to my kicking rote memorization out of my life and to embracing the very process of learning. Rather than trying to give back just what a professor had exposed me to, I began to willingly enter a space where I'd genuinely try to explore and understand the ideas I was offered. I became a more engaged and self-confident learner. As Dr. Burma said, my failures have been my "ticket up and on."

I'd never heard an adult tell the real truth about his life, much less tell the truth about his failures. What a gift to me then and now.

Yet, as I was about to pull out of my auditorium seat, John Burma stopped me with this final thought, "Dave, there's one more thing that I have to pass along to you this afternoon. I've given you a gift, and now I want to give you a promise: I will always believe in you. I believe in you, unconditionally, right now! And, I will always continue to believe in you."

Just as with his stories of failure, Dr. Burma's promise has become an integral part of who I am.

Thinking back on this experience, I realize that in the short-term Dr. Burma encouraged me to stay in college, and he encouraged me across my life to look at my failures head-on and tell myself and others the truth. Even more, to have a trusted adult indicate his unwavering faith in me was a hopeful pledge that made a difference beyond words.

You Call My Name

"Names are the sweetest and most important sound in any language."—Dale Carnegie

Having just completed final exams at the end of my first semester in graduate school at Harvard University, I was absolutely certain that I'd failed three of the four of them. I was distraught. Throughout that semester, I'd been second-guessing myself. *What's a guy like you doing at an Ivy League university where everyone else seems to have come from an elite prep school? They're from wealthy, prestigious families. You're just an impostor! Why don't you get out while it's still possible?*

Yet, I didn't want to disappoint people—my proud family, my professor at Grinnell College who'd worked tirelessly to help secure my entrance to Harvard, even the governor of Iowa who had granted me and one other student a coveted nomination representing the state to the university.

Three university friends who knew of my self-doubts invited me to travel to New York City with them over semester break. They thought that a change of place and pace would somehow turn around my discouragement. "Broadway will cheer you up and you'll have a good time!" They meant well with what they thought were words of encouragement. But I had dug myself a very deep hole.

Still, I accepted their invitation. But instead of taking their advice and losing myself in the excitement of Times Square, within an hour of my arrival I found myself in Manhattan's Morningside Heights neighborhood, kneeling at the prayer rail of the Cathedral of Saint John the Divine. My sadness poured out of me. "Dear God, what's to become of me? What's your will for me?" After a good half hour of pitying myself, I started to exit through a side door when I heard someone call out my name. "Dave, what are you doing here? I can't believe it's you!"

Surprisingly, a good friend from high school, Lincoln Dring, was calling my name. As a second-year student at Union Theological Seminary, he'd arrived at the cathedral on this particular day to interview its dean for a seminary project. In response to his question, I shared something of my woe-is-me state of affairs. He immediately suggested that I be his weekend guest at the seminary dorm. His warm offer encouraged me, as did his words. "I'm so happy to see you, Dave. We'll talk things out over the next few days."

What a spot of good fortune! All my friends had dispersed to follow their own plans. Was this invitation an answer to my prayer?

Over the weekend, Lincoln and I talked about the paths that brought him to seminary and took me to Harvard University to become a teacher. In the process, we recollected the high school teachers who had the strongest impacts upon our directions in life. I don't remember whom Lincoln spoke about, but I do have crystal-clear recall regarding my most influential teacher, my botany teacher, Mr. McMenamin, or, as the students called him, Mr. Mac.

Mr. Mac's artful approach to teaching science and his ways of creating connection with and among adolescents instilled both a love of botany and a sense of being known in his students. Mr. Mac's classroom was organized in the style of a laboratory with four persons to a table, in what he termed "an investigative unit" of "discovery agents and helpmates." The tables competed among each other in friendly ways to be the first in the room, for example, to accurately identify specific plant species. For me, it was unabashed fun!

According to Mr. Mac, there was also a very strong obligation for each student to support others' discoveries and learning. He asked all of us to "mentor" our classmates, a first in my experience as a learner.

For instance, if table #3 solved the day's scientific problem first, then each one of the four students from that table approached one of the other tables and worked with the students at that table until everyone thoroughly understood the solution. Our mentoring followed the precise guidelines Mr. Mac required: We mentors were guides and counselors, working with other students with utmost friendliness and consideration, making sure to use each person's first name. No one was to be left out. Initially, we were to inquire about how the table's members had approached the problem. Then, we were to ask each student to suggest what step might next be taken. Of each student, we were to ask, "What core botany knowledge encourages you to move in that direction?" And, finally, once the group discovered an answer, we mentors were to ask each student, "How do you feel now that you've figured out a solution?" We all not only built our science knowledge, but also came to know each other exceedingly well.

I told Lincoln, "I was bursting with feelings of accomplishment in Mr. Mac's class. I always felt joyful as I trooped through the doorway of Room 110. Somehow, I felt completely known and appreciated in that classroom. I think we all felt that way."

In addition, Mr. Mac distinguished himself by inviting each of his students in small groups to go on optional botanical field trips on Saturday mornings. Mr. Mac remained a practicing scientist and his offer to gather with him, literally and figuratively, around a scientific question that was of interest to him brought us all in relation to each other around a bit of botany. We served as his willing apprentices, probably in part because during those informal events, our person-to-person relationships deepened as he often encouraged us to discuss our interests outside of school.

"So, Dave, who is the Harvard professor who most reminds you of Mr. Mac?" asked Lincoln.

After a few moments I declared, "John Gaus is my favorite Harvard professor." Lincoln asked me why I felt that way. Collecting my thoughts, I shared these ideas with him: "John Gaus teaches a course called American Regional Politics. I find it fascinating. The regional area that he knows like the back of his hand is comprised of the eighteen northernmost counties in

Wisconsin, a section of the state known as 'the cutover region,' where thousands of conifer trees were cut to make farming possible.

"Even more," I went on, "I so appreciate the interest that Dr. Gaus takes in each student and his or her region. Starting on the first day and throughout the semester, our assignment was to write about our home region. Where is it? What is its history? What are the politics and the most important issues in the region that we call home? And, if we were on the Planning Committee for that region, what would we suggest as next positive steps to be taken there? I had fun with that assignment. I was engaged and curious.

"As the term went on, each of us met one-on-one with Professor Gaus. At that meeting, his goal was, in his own words, 'to learn the fit, the match, of the student to his or her region.' I don't remember the particular questions I was asked during the hour-long session, just my feelings of being at ease as we discussed what I'd learned about my region. We also spoke about my possible future path in ways that felt like a talk between friends, but of different ages and status. As a result of that conversation, I felt that John Gaus knew me, and I knew him."

I further told Lincoln: "Many late afternoons, as I walked back to my room following a Regional Politics class, I pondered the question, 'Do all of us in this class feel well known and recognized?' Each day he calls on one of us, beginning the class with someone's name and the welcoming words: 'Good afternoon, Dave, what would you like to share about today's topic? What's at the heart of the matter for you? What's important about this afternoon's issue?' When Dr. Gaus calls each of our names and inquires of us in this way, we all relax. With him, I again feel recognized and appreciated."

My weekend in New York City was a gift, just as my Harvard friends suggested it would be. But the gift was not received by being immersed in the excitement of the bright lights of Times Square. Rather, the gift was given to me through a "chance" encounter with a high school friend. I had been overwhelmed with doubt and had forgotten my true self during my first semester at Harvard. Lincoln called me back home to my best self. Not only did he offer me his time and his compassion, which comforted and heartened me, but also he helped me remember who I was as a successful learner.

When I returned to Harvard and checked the posted course grades, I discovered to my surprise that I'd done quite well on those final exams. What I'd written had resulted in three grades of A- and even one of A+. When the examination "blue books" were returned to me, these words from Professor Gaus caught my eye and heart: "Dave, you are a man of the land. May you always receive comfort from the land."

Each of the key people in this essay—Lincoln, Professor Gaus, and Mr. Mac—called my name in his own way. All three literally used my name. But even more, I felt each of them recognized me and helped me to recognize myself. Being recognized and appreciated for who a person is—now, to me, that's the ultimate encouragement.

Calling

You call my name
long after it has been forgotten
by all who say they love me.

You touch me
at the core of my being
while others have left,
believing that there is nothing there.

You breathe love
into the vessel of my heart
and fill it with warmth and tenderness
even as others take from me
my last
gasping
breath.

You hold me in a sacred space,
honoring me for who I am,
while others honor me
for who they want me to be.

You call my name,
and I am moved to tears
because I too had forgotten.

—Daniel H. Kim

VOCATION'S EARLY DAYS

The Blue Bicycle Summer

"When you do things from your soul"

In the Eye of the Storm

The Blue Bicycle Summer

Reciprocal acts of welcome encourage the re-creation of a newly desegregated school community.

"Look, here he comes now. He's coming to our house. And he's on that blue bike. Do you think he'll stay for lunch?"

When asked that question by her brother, Natasha thought for a moment and then went into the kitchen to see what was on the shelves. "We've got some pork and beans. Do you think that would make a good lunch for the new principal?" Natasha called out.

"Anything will do. And let's give him a Coke," Tony said to his sister and the collection of seven other neighborhood kids that had gathered on the porch of their home near the intersection of Lake and Dodge.

Natasha turned to me when I pulled up to her house. "Hello Mr. Principal. I just knew you'd come to my house. My mama said you'd be too busy to come all this way. But I just knew you'd come. I saw you coming from a long way off. I've been waiting for you for so long. Our mama's not home, but we've got lunch ready. Mama said it would be just fine for us to give you lunch in case you came to our house. She cleaned up the house, just in case. Mr. Principal, Tony and I want to know, do you like pork and beans?"

The year was 1967. Numerous petitions, church and synagogue meetings, community organizing efforts, and committee discussions within the school system had all focused intensely on the desegregation of the Evanston, Illinois, schools. Natasha and Tony's elementary school, Foster, had been closed the year before as a part of that citywide effort. A citizen's panel had determined it was morally unjustifiable to maintain neighborhood schools based on race, while also claiming to be an accepting place for all people. (At the time, Evanston was a city mostly comprised of separate Black and white communities.) Prior to desegregation, Foster School had been a community center with a rich history of engagement and culture and thus, its loss was one of the unfortunate outcomes of desegregation. Previously a primarily African American school, Foster was transformed into a laboratory school, accepting applications from all across town. Although local children could apply to the new Martin Luther King, Jr. Lab School, many of the children from the old neighborhood school would be traveling to outlying schools like the all-white Willard School in the somewhat conservative far northwest corner of Evanston.

Just prior to 1967, I was happily serving as Dean of Students at a local junior college. My career path took me toward providing supportive campus-based student services. I fully expected that in the future I'd look for a similar position at a larger four-year university, perhaps at a place like Northwestern University or the University of Illinois. At the same time, I had become involved in the civil rights movement, marching in my community for greater housing opportunities for African American families.

So I found myself surprised when friends began encouraging me to apply for the newly-opened principal's job at Willard School. "You could make a contribution," these friends told me. "Because you live in northwest Evanston and your house is only a block from the school, you'd be a neighborhood insider. Your presence would say to the locals, 'You have nothing to fear.'" My friends also believed my experience with the civil rights issues of the day could help me bring sensitivity and effectiveness to the work that needed to be done to extend a sincere welcome as Black kids arrived at an all-white school and in co-creating a place of belonging and learning with their families.

My friends persuaded me. *Perhaps*, I thought to myself, *it would be all right to set my intended career on the sideline for a while. This Willard job will allow me to do something even more important with my life.* What I didn't know at the time was the depth of my calling to a life of bringing people together. Had I understood myself more fully when considering my shift in career plans, I could have imagined that the Willard School principal's position was truly close to the heart of things for me. I'd always deeply cared about matters related to inclusion, and I loathed that some folks experienced extreme alienation. My deep gladness, my passion, came when I had the chance to encourage people to feel at home. If only I'd known then what I know now, I would have rejoiced that my deep gladness was about to meet the world's deep need, as Frederick Buechner has put it, and I would soon fall in love with my work at Willard School.

So there I was, the newly appointed principal, pedaling my bicycle to deliver classroom assignments in late July. This approach came as a result of the set of directions given to me by the outgoing principal. "When it comes to letting parents know about their child's teacher for the next year, here's how you do it," I was told. "Once you've determined the class assignments, get the information onto postcards addressed to parents. Wait until the Friday before Labor Day, and on that day, after the last pickup of the day, dump all of the postcards in the mailbox right in front of Carl's gas station. That way, the post office people will pick up the cards on Saturday morning, and they'll be delivered on the day after Labor Day. Because school starts on the Wednesday after Labor Day and there will be no one at school on Tuesday since everyone will be attending back-to-school meetings at the central office, there will be no opportunity for parents to fuss and fume about their child's assignment. This method cuts way back on the grief factor for the principal. If you remember nothing else that I tell you, be sure to remember this, and you'll be off to a great start with your new work. Now, are you sure you're going to remember?"

Well, I remembered, and I was appalled! Especially that year, when lots of people would be new to Willard as a recently desegregated school, it would be just awful for parents to receive news about their child's classroom assignment in the way described by my predecessor. I began to wonder how I could best ensure that everyone felt included. And how could I have some fun while making sure each family and their children felt invited and welcomed? My blue bicycle summer resulted from that wondering.

I didn't know how these blue bicycle deliveries would go. I'd never done anything like this before and I imagined that families might well have a lot to say about their hopes and, especially, their concerns. But no matter the neighborhood, everyone seemed to appreciate these bicycle deliveries. Families and children continuing at Willard School, who'd received their assignments under a previous system, thought it was a novel and welcome approach. Some of those nearby neighbors started greeting me with, "Hello, Doctor Dave!" In the Foster School neighborhood, I felt warmly welcomed again and again, as if I were a new neighbor. The families extended me grace and invited me into their community. Over the six-week delivery period, I was treated to breakfasts, lunches, suppers, and what seemed like gallons of coffee and Coke. Getting out each day encouraged my feeling that I was trying to do something in this uncertain situation and making important progress in connecting with the children and families I'd be working with in the coming months. Of course, I thought it likely that significant challenges lay ahead, but at least we'd met each other on the families' home grounds with reciprocal goodwill.

Both new and continuing families reported their appreciation that the principal had taken action to pave the way for as smooth a transition as possible. The welcoming process encouraged *all* the kids and their families to know that they were recognized and accepted into this new environment. The new kids and families reported a sense of feeling recognized as part of the school community, which also introduced a reservoir of talented parent-leaders. Family members new to our school community eagerly volunteered to work in classrooms and the lunchroom, as well as on the playground; assist with neighborhood meetings; help with carpools when the bus broke down; and do anything they could to help create a new school community. A story and photograph in the *Chicago Tribune* brought citywide recognition, sparking encouragement in the entire school community.

I believe that from the beginning we came together as a school community wanting to make desegregation work. But the real work of co-creating a place of mutual belonging and learning was yet to come. The blue bicycle summer had helped us begin that journey together.

When you do things from your soul,
you feel a river in you,
a joy.

—Rumi

In the Eye of the Storm

In a time of community crisis, a small leadership team finds trust among its members as a way to encourage positive action.

A divisive political storm thundered over the community of Evanston, Illinois, in the late 1960s when desegregation plans sought to end the segregation of educational systems based on race and unequal resources. Those plans intended to create more equitable educational opportunities for all children. In the case of Evanston, this aim meant that all of the K-8 school attendance areas were redrawn so that the enrollment of its African American children at each school was more evenly distributed to range from 17 to 25 percent.

Almost everyone along the tree-lined streets of this close-in Chicago suburb was affected by the school busing that was necessary to achieve this target. Whether you were a student reassigned from a formerly all-Black school or a white parent whose child was learning "relationship skills" in a newly desegregated school or simply a long-term resident of this community, you were at the very least aware of the turbulence in the Evanston Public Schools.

Having a background in sociology I found it curious, but perhaps not surprising, that many community members and parents didn't bring up, and even seemed to avoid, the underlying issues of race and the purposes of education. Instead, many of them directed their intense ire toward the school district superintendent, Gregory Coffin. Rightly or wrongly, the clash of those tempestuous times seemed to sound the loudest when many of the anti-desegregation citizens focused on the leadership style of the superintendent. They declared him to be "cut-throat, abrasive, and a non-listener." Others who supported desegregation of the schools found him to be their champion of change. "He is able to see what needs doing," his advocates would say, "and he does what needs doing."

Many persons would have said the school desegregation process in Evanston came down to the contentious struggle regarding whether the superintendent should go or stay. The drama of this struggle took place over months and almost nightly on the stage of the city's Unitarian Church, a building that could hold more people than the K-8 school district's auditorium.

At eight o'clock on many evenings, the school board would convene there in public session. Although there were usually other items on the agenda, the *raison d'être* of the school board's attention centered on the tenure of Coffin and usually ran well past midnight. Often, the question on the street the next day turned out to be, "Did you attend the shouting match last night?"

Coffin was so completely engulfed in what he called the "struggle of my lifetime" that he had little time to orchestrate and oversee the operations of the Evanston Public Schools. Such activities were left to Joe Hill, the Associate Superintendent; Frank Christensen, the Personnel Director; Ken Orton, the Director of Business Affairs; and me. At the time, I was the Director of Curriculum and Instruction. We all supported the desegregation effort. Basically, the four of us together coordinated and managed that 11,000-student school district for the better part of a year.

In truth, the district didn't have a single leader. Rather, this group of four became "the superintendent."

The four of us started every day at 7 a.m. with what we called a "state of our world" meeting. We were exhausted from the usual late-hour turmoil of the night before and often began with a couple of minutes of grumbling. Then, we would settle down and set up the agenda for the day. We determined which schools each one of us would visit; we divided up the correspondence that needed response; we made a list of who would call whom. In an effort to maintain and advance regular matters of curriculum and instruction, we rated the concerns of teachers from one to five, identifying those that were most critical to move forward. We sought to provide a central office presence and assure that the day was dedicated to the young people in our charge.

And then we would leave the superintendent's office with this pledge: We will move through the day with a "servant's heart." We would be at the beck and call of the people we served. We would do what needed to be done on behalf of the young people, the teachers, and the community. We vowed never to say a disparaging word about anyone, including the members of our team.

Unexpectedly, this period became one of the first times I experienced deep trust in my colleagues. In fact, we four trusted one another completely. There were no lies. There was no deception. There were no exaggerations. There were no partial truths. Nothing was hush-hush. There were no "arrangements." What felt like madness swirled around us, but in an atmosphere of trust, we experienced a kind of pure calmness. We felt confident. We lived with grounded hope and realistic encouragement that the quality of the school district could be and was being sustained, even enhanced.

Among the four of us, there was no panic, there was no tension, and there was no despair. It was a time of telling the truth and, refreshingly, it was a time of laughter. As I recall those days, a smile comes to my face; I remember that year as a time when I had a great deal of fun on a leadership team. At the end of the day, when we again came together to review our activities, we joked with one another, we reveled in one another's victories, and we somehow found the "crazy calamities" of our failures and mistakes to be cause for a good belly laugh.

How is it possible that amid the chaos of what we called "the Coffin cacophony" we had a positive, peaceful, and productive experience? And why, in the midst of that chaos, would trust and laughter find such a comfortable home?

Well, for one thing, we felt we had no choice but to help make good things happen for those in our care. In our situation, there was little room for wondering, worry, or waiting for others to make decisions. Indeed, the political battle spinning around us was not of our doing, was beyond our control, and was at times beyond our understanding.

And then there was the makeup of our leadership team. Ken Orton was a true-blue kind of guy. Of course, he knew the numbers and so I called him Careful Ken. He was good. And he was more than good; Ken was also keenly and genuinely interested in everyone. Whether it was a teacher, school board or community member, Ken took that person seriously and did whatever was necessary to thoroughly answer their questions. Ken loved the work he did, but I believe he loved people more.

Many in the Black community considered Joe Hill the soul of Evanston, where he'd grown up. He stood at the heart of the Black community in a town that was, at the time, referred to as primarily a Black and white city. He had an infectious sense of humor, a loving manner with all of the children, and the respect and admiration of citizens.

Frank Christensen was known for his legendary practices in human relations. For instance, when a kindergarten child was preparing to step off to school for the first time, Frank would visit that child's home a few days before, spending a substantial bit of time with that child and the family. Teachers received similar gifts of Frank's attention. To this day, Frank Christensen is my ideal educator. He was a positive and cheerful symbol of encouragement to all.

Of course, I did my part. I was "the new kid" within the team. But I gave it my all.

Overall, we four teammates shared a mutual goal of encouraging public trust in the schools, reflected respect for each other, made information transparent among us, maintained a positive outlook, possessed a can-do spirit and willingly gave ourselves to the endeavor for the common good. Because of all these traits and dynamics we found the gift of trust in our midst.

Remarkably, I learned that it's possible to develop and live with trust in a time of crisis, a time when I, and perhaps others, might have thought that trust would not flourish. And thus, I felt tremendously encouraged to bring my very best efforts both to the team and to the cause of creating more equitable educational opportunities for all children.

This group became one of the most encouraging teams I've ever been involved in. Perhaps we had found ourselves in the perfect setting for trust, together in the eye of the storm.

THE WISCONSIN FARM

Encouraging, the Rossow Way

"We live by encouragement..."

Encouraging, the Rossow Way

An elderly neighbor encourages by way of surprise.

I looked down from my ladder on hearing the startling sound of a lawnmower disturbing the stillness of that bright October day. Our family had just purchased an abandoned farm in Wisconsin. Inside the house, trash piles filled the corners, the propane heater required repair, and all the floors and walls needed to be stripped and repainted. As much work as there was to be done inside, the property surrounding the house revealed piles of wood and old tires, as well as a rusted-out car. The fence posts fell unevenly, with locations of broken barbed wire. The waterline to the house cried for repair and cleaning out so that water could safely be consumed. The grass grew knee-high. I felt both eager and overwhelmed. I knew I had to give the 138-year-old farmhouse a long-overdue coat of paint before the autumn freeze set in. From the rungs of the ladder, I saw a spry old man hacking away at the knee-high grass closest to the house. "I'm your neighbor," he said. "Nothing to worry about. I'm just cutting your grass."

That was my introduction to "Rossow," probably the happiest, most encouraging person I've ever known. The letters on his mailbox said A.G. Rossow, and I think his first name was Avolt, but when anyone asked his first name, he said, "I've always been just 'Rossow,' even to my wife, and I'm not going to change it now."

Rossow possessed an ageless quality that endeared him to hundreds of mid-Wisconsin residents. When I first met him, he'd just retired at age 70 from his job as a dishwasher at the local Baptist retreat center and occupied his time from early morning until late at night tending to the chores around his small farm, as well as helping his friends from miles around do their outdoor work. Building fences, harvesting hay, sawing wood, or cutting the grass, no job seemed too big, too small, or too difficult for Rossow.

Everything that Rossow did was done with joy and laughter. He loved to share stories and jokes. Often he got to laughing so hard while telling his own stories that he had to hold his sides or sit down on the ground. Sometimes he couldn't finish the story because his sides hurt so much. He was a loveable old man, twice my age, and a joy to be with.

Rossow was an adjudicator of justice; he possessed and encouraged a powerful sense of fairness, often asking the simple question, "Is it fair?" One night, he surprised me by knocking on my kitchen door at about 10 o'clock. I knew something was terribly wrong since he was always in bed by 9:30. "Come out," he said, "let's talk in my truck." He immediately began scolding me, "It's about that hay you sold to Bob. I counted the tiers in the barn and checked on the condition of the hay. It should have been a lower price, son. You overcharged Bob. It isn't right, so let's correct it right now. I'll drive you to Bob's so it can be done with. You'll sleep better tonight, and the news you'll bring to Bob will be encouraging to him." Off we drove, the realization of what had just occurred trailing somewhat behind the pace of the truck. Wow! As a result, and somewhat to my surprise, I later became fast-friends with Bob.

Rossow also often inquired, "Anything you need?" He shared all that he owned—a post-hole digger, apples, his little green truck—except for his John Deere tractor, his baby! "It's a way to encourage people," he said. Mostly, he shared his time, labor, and goodwill and, in doing so, he encouraged me to believe that I had assistance in my huge project with my new farm, that I wasn't in it by myself, that I had gained a helpful neighbor and new friend.

I deeply appreciated Rossow's everyday practices of encouraging people, no strings attached. Often I think back to that October day and the ladder and the lawnmower. As the years went by, I realized that "Nothing to worry about, I'm just cutting your grass" was not simply an introductory kindness, but shorthand for Rossow's way of encouraging.

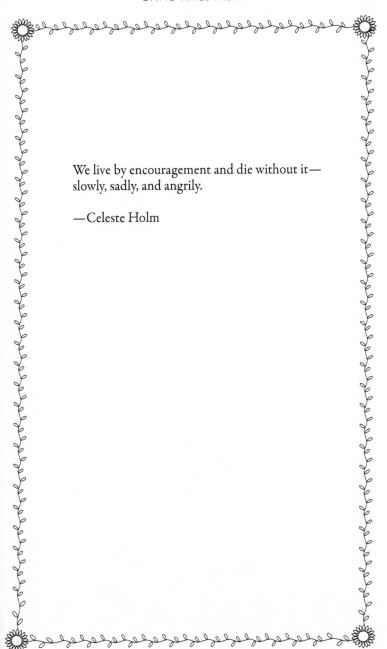

We live by encouragement and die without it—
slowly, sadly, and angrily.

—Celeste Holm

MEDICAL ENCOUNTERS

A Song Strong in My Soul

"The Quiet Place"

Luck of the Draw

Out of the Blue

My Physician Is a Dinosaur

A Song Strong in My Soul

A night nurse encourages a new way of listening.

In 1982, I was in the front row at Centennial Hall in Juneau, Alaska. A local artist was singing the melody, "Without A Song." The music and its lyrics touched me to my very core. That tune had always made my heart sing.

But something was not right that evening. Either the vocalist was forgetting some words, or the background singers were skipping notes. Or maybe the sound system was faulty. Somehow, in some way, the various artists in front of me on stage had eliminated all of the high notes!

For the entire week following the disappointing performance I was troubled about the recital. I thought about writing a "one-star review" to the local paper, expressing my dismay. But then the disappearance of high notes occurred again, this time as I was listening to my preferred FM radio station. Whoa!

Eventually, I realized the problem might not be "out there" but "in here." So, I embarked on what became a six-month journey in and out of physicians' offices. I hoped they could solve the case of the missing high notes.

After yet another visit to a well-recommended medical wizard brought no clear diagnosis, I returned to my regular clinic another day. There a nurse practitioner greeted me with these words, "Follow me, we're going to do an MRI of your brain." I wanted the information that an MRI might provide, but I was scared about the actual mechanism I'd be required to undergo, it being very new equipment at the time.

Within a few hours, I sat down with a neurosurgeon and viewed a brain tumor the size of a large tangerine. "Whoa!" I said.

"It certainly deserves a whoa," he said.

A sixteen-hour surgery followed several weeks later. As a result, I initially lost my abilities to talk with ease (for one month), to walk except with great effort (for two months), and to run (for six months), an activity I'd pursued regularly. I permanently lost my ability to close my right eye. The other eye has lost its visual acuity at the rate of a percent each year. And, almost immediately, my right ear went dead and has stayed that way. On that day back in 1983, my auditory nerve connections suffered substantial accidental damage in the course of the surgery. But there was a part of me that was to flourish: my heart.

I was in the hospital for twenty-three days. As it turned out, Jill served as my nurse every night for my entire stay in the hospital. I don't know how that was arranged, or why, but it was clear to me from the start, Jill was my angel. Jill was truly a messenger of encouragement.

Jill always engaged me in conversation. On the first night, she asked, "What must you return to, and what can you throw overboard?" I wanted to return to running 10k races, and I needed to figure out a different way to shave the new zigzags of my face. After the first couple of nights, the questions turned to favorite things. "What song do you deeply love?" Jill inquired. At the time, my favorite tune was still "Without A Song." So the next night Jill produced a portable listening device. She placed an earphone on my good ear, turned up the volume, and I listened to Willie Nelson's voice: "When things go wrong a man ain't got a friend / Without a song." The words brought tears to both Jill and to me that night.

Over the next week, Jill asked me about other favorite things—my Wisconsin farm, canoeing in the Canadian Quetico Provincial Park, playing my harmonicas, and so much more. But soon thereafter, she invited me to return to my love of music. "So, David, let's go back to your favorite song lyrics in 'Without A Song.' Do you remember that significant line you shared with me earlier? I'll sing it for you. 'I'll get along as long as a song is strong in my soul.'"

We were both very still for many minutes after that melodic

interlude. And then Jill reminded me that earlier in the week I had told her that music taps into my heart. "Well," she said. "So, now, you'll be our Heart Man. You will listen with your heart. And, as you listen, you will hear, of course, your favorite songs, and you will hear the deeply loved and cherished songs of many others. You'll hear their soul songs."

At the time of Jill's charge to me, my first reaction was one of surprise and then puzzlement. Later, the skills I learned through speech and hearing rehabilitation helped me function again in the world of hearing people, but I found that without the usual physical process to help me hear, I began to turn more and more to listening in other ways. My ears have considerable difficulty perceiving sounds these days; however, my heart has become a deeper, more trustworthy source of hearing. There's a song strong in my soul. I hear my song and other people's too. I listen with my heart.

The Quiet Place

It's been good
this journey towards
the quiet place

Adventures
here and there
good friends
along the way

A few missteps
but mostly
gift on gift

Noise
the hurtful intruder
pushes in
from time to time
brings pain and suffering

But it's really quiet now
clear soft humming
sounds from yesterday
sweet music of today

It's so peaceful here
every whisper's heard
deep within
the quiet place

— David Hagstrom

Luck of the Draw

Learning to live with life's circumstances clarifies my life purpose.

This being human is a guest house.
Every morning a new arrival.
A joy, a depression, a meanness,
some momentary awareness comes
as an unexpected visitor.
Welcome and entertain them all!
Even if they are a crowd of sorrows,
who violently sweep your house
empty of its furniture,
still, treat each guest honorably.
He may be clearing you out
for some new delight.
The dark thought, the shame, the malice.
meet them at the door laughing and invite them in.
Be grateful for whatever comes,
because each has been sent
as a guide from beyond.

—Rumi

As I was beginning an extensive recovery period following my brain tumor, I asked my neurosurgeon the "why me?" question: "Dr. Ciric, why did I develop this brain tumor?" His initial response surprised me; his follow-up explanation was enigmatic.

Ivan Ciric, M.D. looked me in the eye and declared without emotion, "Luck of the draw." I was stunned speechless. He continued, "You did nothing wrong. We can't pinpoint the reason this complicated situation paid you a visit. But here's something that I've learned from my experience with patients over the years: life is about mastering our circumstances. And, as we do so, we find our true purpose."

At first, I simply could not grasp the possibility of adjusting to my predicament. How could a loss of most of my hearing, an inability to close my right eye, and vocal chord dysfunction lead me to some form of clarification about my life? Preposterous! This prospect felt unrealistic and unattainable.

And so, having dismissed my physician's prognostication as merely a dose of well intentioned, but ineffective, encouragement, my recovery proceeded. In the care of a superb team of health practitioners at the Northwestern University Speech and Hearing Clinic, I relearned how to speak. One of the team members, Jamie, even gave me singing lessons to strengthen my voice. She mentioned that as we age, we may forget some language, but in singing, the words of a song are rarely forgotten. "Sing your heart out, David. Your vocal chords will love it!" Jamie taught me how to lip read. And, she further offered me practical tips about how to live life fully in my new non-hearing world. For instance, placing myself in a corner would help diminish somewhat the cacophony of many people speaking at once in a room. Doing so, Jamie declared, would put me more in charge of the situation. She was a true envoy of encouragement and real cheerleader.

Jamie worked with me in a frank and direct manner. "Just tell folks you have a completely dead right ear and your left ear will soon be joining the other one in experiencing complete silence. Have a little fun with your disability, David! It'll make your life a lot more interesting." The first time she said that to me, I was disturbed. *Why is she telling me this? I don't need to hear this.* But as the years have gone by, I've come to understand and live into Jamie's perspective, which has added a light touch to a difficult situation.

I loved my Speech and Hearing friends. They gave me the will and the skill to get on with my life.

After six months of significant post-surgery healing, I was ready to return to my work as an educator. As a college professor at the University of Alaska I taught on-campus courses and also traveled to small villages across the state to both teach courses and to visit local schools. I liked the teaching, and I enjoyed offering encouragement to the conscientious rural schoolteachers. I found these visits to be both exciting and rewarding.

Immersing myself in teaching and travels helped me to somewhat forget my own disabilities. But, interestingly, I found myself noticing others with health incapacities. They were everywhere! I observed those who walked haltingly and connected easily with them. I often spotted those with limited eyesight, and I was keenly aware of persons who were struggling with their hearing. Those with facial droops characteristic of a brain tumor or stroke patients were easy for me to identify. I felt not so alone. I made friendly contact with them whenever they passed my way. If I did nothing else, I tipped my cap to them. I tried not to intrude in their lives; however, I was deeply touched by their presence. I simply wanted what was best for them. My incapacity helped me appreciate theirs.

Within a few years following my surgery, I realized this awareness of persons with special needs was expanding. I found myself wanting what was best for literally everyone who crossed my path. I wondered, does a sense of compassion for others become more developed with the passing of years? As we become more mature, do we become more compassionate? Or, does experiencing a life-threatening encounter groom us for a more compassionate way of being with others? For a while, I was unsure but now I realize both can be true. At the time, I simply liked who I was becoming.

Then, one morning a full decade after my surgery, I finally awoke to the realization that, maybe, I was beginning to master the circumstances that came my way as a result of my brain tumor. Because I was beginning to learn how to be in my modified life, I was being invited to be more aware of the circumstances and needs of others. What had begun as a feeling of relief that I wasn't alone in my state of disability, moved into compassion, and later, as that compassion began to seek a more active expression, into encouragement.

I continue to learn how to master my own circumstances, even now thirty-five years after my surgery. I've made progress. But, there's more to learn. No matter how much more I need to master, I believe I've found my true purpose. My neurosurgeon, Dr. Ciric, was as wise as he was skilled. It's taken me a while to appreciate what he shared with me early in my recovery. As I persist with my learning, my purpose is becoming crystal clear: I am a messenger of encouragement. Thanks, Dr. Ciric.

Out of the Blue

Navigating the seas of life, a medical emergency brings unexpected encouragement.

We were in bed. Karen was reading to me from the latest Louise Penny mystery, and it was about time to turn out the lights. And then, I felt some liquid beneath me. How strange! It was a small pool of bright red blood. Feeling surprised and wondering what was going on, I went immediately to the bathroom, and by the time I got there, blood was gushing out. Karen, feeling alarmed, insisted we call 911. Out of the blue, a storm had blown across the sea of my otherwise calm life.

The ambulance arrived at our front door in roughly five minutes. The gurney had difficulty negotiating our narrow front steps and gate, so the EMTs helped me walk down the stairs and we made our way to the stretcher at the back door of the ambulance. I was lifted into the brightly lit core of the emergency vehicle, which was decorated with blinking multi-colored lights, it being the day after Christmas. Playing softly in the background was a soothing version of the hymn "Silent Night." Although blood was pouring out of me, I felt comforted.

Within twelve minutes, we arrived at Good Samaritan Hospital's Emergency Department. Without much fuss or bother, I was taken to an exam room and transferred from the gurney to a hospital bed. In an instant, the triage nurse, Dawn, began asking me questions: Had this ever happened before? No. Had I been constipated in the past few days? Yes, somewhat. Was I on a blood thinner? Plavix? Coumadin? Eliquis? No, no, no! I thought the questions would never end as all the while, I was spurting out life liquid. Now I was feeling alarmed myself and these questions seemed to be interfering with getting the bleeding stopped ASAP. "Thank goodness you're not taking a blood thinner," Dawn told me. "That makes this kind of situation even more difficult to stop." Then, Dawn moved on to asking about my blood type, which did seem especially relevant in this situation. I didn't know, so the team took a blood sample, and more quickly than I would have imagined, they proclaimed, "It's A negative."

Within moments, I was poked and an intravenous line was positioned in my left arm. That move came none too soon. Dawn had stepped out to talk with the EMTs, when suddenly I began to feel dizzy. It was clear to me that something was desperately wrong. Looking at my pale lips and chalky skin tone, Karen shouted, "We need some help in here!" I felt helpless and out of control. I felt like death was at the edge of the room. Apparently, I was beginning to go into shock.

Rushing back into the cubicle, Dawn took one look at me and tilted the head of the bed downwards. She lifted up my knees so that they reached back toward my face.

I prayed silently. *Please, God, not now, not now.*

Dawn told one of the team to immediately request units of A negative blood. Finally, those units arrived and Dawn hooked me up. Yet, I continued to bleed. Blood in, blood out.

Before much more time elapsed, I was taken into the Intensive Care Unit (ICU). There, the on-duty intensivist physician, Dr. Brandon Young, an internal medicine specialist and head of the ICU, came to my bedside. "I don't wish for you to be alarmed; however, your situation is quite serious. I've called in a superb gastroenterologist, Dr. Jeffrey Buehler. He'll give you a colonoscopy. He'll find out what's going on."

My ICU nurse, Liz, put her hand on my tummy. "David, I know this prepping for the colonoscopy isn't going to be pleasant, but are you ready to get started so you can get it over with?"

Liz and I made a game of it. At the conclusion of each glass of the less-than-tasty liquid laxative I consumed, Liz put a hash mark on the white board in my room. "Atta boy, David," was her rallying call. I did my very best. When the container was finally emptied, there were twenty hash marks on the board. I was secretly proud of myself and Liz declared that she'd never had a patient who'd completed such prep in four hours. Later, the attending gastroenterologist, Dr. Meghan Nesmith, declared, "You've broken the record. Fastest prep ever. You did it. Good for you!"

By then it was 6 a.m. I waited. And I waited some more and I bled, with periods of no bleeding between gushes.

Around noon, Dr. Buehler, the gastroenterologist, performed the colonoscopy but was unable to see or detect the source(s) of bleeding, due to the continued bleeding itself. I was wheeled back into the ICU, to be greeted by my nurse, Emily. She said, "These diverticular bleeds often resolve on their own." Without complaining, she and others on the team of nurses continued to collect blood and clean me up. I began to worry whether my situation was not one of those that would take care of itself. I felt increasingly anxious and was afraid that I'd literally bleed to death.

Emily left the room after four bedpans and soon Dr. Young re-appeared about 6 p.m. He said calmly, "The bleeding isn't stopping on its own. So, David, we have a plan for what's next. We're going to use a procedure that calls for interventional radiology (IR) and I'm going to bring in Dr. Semonsen and his team. They are the best."

Dr. Young's straightforward manner combined with the sense of confidence he conveyed without arrogance, communicated that he knew what he was doing, which eased both my physical and psychological pain. He asked for my permission to call "the best IR guy," who would assemble his team with the goal of locating and ending the bleeding. Dr. Young noted that if the IR procedure failed, the surgical removal of the total "bleed territory," would be necessary. Hoping to avoid that totally unappealing alternative, I told him, "Let's do it."

Wait time in the ICU is dreamlike. By 7 p.m., Dr. Kevin Semonsen had assembled his twelve-member interventional radiology team; his assistants, nurses and other medical professionals had all been at home, relaxing into dinner and their evening plans. Soon, nurses Candace and Sarah arrived to wheel me through the mostly deserted hallways into what seemed to me to be a huge, cavernous, well-lit "surgical theater." On entering the room, I was awe-struck by the radiology apparatus and the other technological contraptions mostly positioned on the edges of the enormous space. But, of course, I arrived in the space lying flat on a hospital bed; my viewing angle was distorted.

Immediately, I was propped up into a rather peculiar operating position. My tummy—that's what the team kept calling my physical "area of critical interest"—was positioned to face two very different radiology instruments. One was shaped in the form of an arc. This instrument moved constantly from left to right and back again. The other instrument was box-like. It moved in and out towards my tummy and then retreated. Dr. Semonsen was positioned at a location somehow lower than me, and to my right. It all seemed peculiar, but it must have been strategic. Who was I to wonder or worry? I was here to be given new life.

I was given only mild anesthesia to very gently sedate me. Dr. Semonsen wanted to be able to talk with me during the procedure. His first words were, "David, it's extremely important that you do not move for the minutes or hours of this complicated procedure. You are bleeding from multiple sites. It's going to take my concentration and your motionlessness to make this a success. So, my new friend, here we go. Hold on tight!" Indeed, I actually held on to the handles before me.

For the next two hours, I did my very best to remain perfectly motionless. I used a meditation technique. On the calm breath in I said in my head the word *be*, and on each calm breath out I used the word *still*. As it turned out, my partner during this otherworldly episode didn't talk to me all that much. I'd hear an occasional, "You're being very still, David, keep it up." I also heard a lot of words he uttered to himself or to his assistant: "So many places! This is difficult beyond belief!"

I watched the clock on the far wall and into the second hour,

I began to think of Dr. Semonsen as an artist and my wizard. He meticulously inserted metal coils into each and every bleeding blood vessel using a sheath opening in my groin area. The coils embolized the areas; they caused the blood to clot up in the mass of the coil in the way of the flow. So, he was closing up a specific site inside of me instead of opening a specific spot inside of me, like the stents that had been previously placed in an artery to allow my blood to flow more easily. It required a detailed, painstaking, and vigilant effort on his part. I was awestruck!

At the conclusion of the procedure, Dr. Semonsen informed me that a total of nine separate coils had been inserted in the various affected blood vessels. He said that getting all the coils in place was "touch and go for a while," but "we did it." Then, he quickly departed.

I've expressed my gratitude to most of the participants in this medical extravaganza; however, I have yet to thank Dr. Semonsen. The word "on the street" of the ICU was that my night propped up in front his numerous radiology instruments gave him one of his most difficult challenges. Hearing that, I want even more to offer my thanks.

Within about twenty-four hours after I first felt the bedtime bleeding, I had almost gone into shock and received blood transfusions, been poked repeatedly in my hands, arms and even neck in attempts to locate the best or, at times, only intravenous entry points, prepped for and experienced a colonoscopy—while still losing blood—and finally, underwent the intricate IR embolization procedure that ceased the bleeding. Now, we would see if those coils would do their job over the rest of the night.

Nurses Sarah and Candace wheeled me back to my ICU home away from home. The coming nighttime hours turned into the most difficult time for me in this entire episode. I had become weary and worried to my very core.

I felt very anxious and I pleaded with my nurse, Emily, "I need more blood! I feel like I did before in the Emergency Department. Isn't there something that you can do, Emily?" Gently, tenderly, Emily repeatedly conveyed the same message to me, "David, your physicians believe that you have received enough blood at this time. You just need to find the way to rest. What might I do for you to bring you some calm moments?" I could not find calm.

By the time of the 4 a.m. blood draw, I was feeling a bit less wound up. I looked over and saw Karen curled up in a lounge chair that the nursing team had brought in for her. She'd slept in my ICU room the last two nights. I found myself overcome with emotion at that moment. Karen and I were as one in this adventure. With every coil installation, every new transfusion connection, and every poke and prod, I would groan, and then in the core of my being, I would hear her groan. In my heart, Karen and I were but one organism during this bizarre escapade. That was both a comfort and anguish for me. I was so fortunate that the love of my life was so interconnected with me during this challenging time. But why, oh why, did she have to go through all of this pain?

With the arrival of the 7:30 a.m. nursing shift, I was given some good news. Aman, my day nurse announced, "Hi there, David, sorry you had such a tough night. Dr. Young left word that you are improving. There's been no further bleeding. The late-night stats are encouraging." In addition to receiving the positive information, I liked Aman a lot.

By this time in my adventure, probably twenty or more physicians, nurses, nursing assistants, and other health professionals had assisted me. I was completed impressed with all of them. Of course, I got to know the nursing staff quite well and found them, without exception, to be attentive, knowledgeable, articulate, thoughtful, considerate, understanding, respectful, careful, and caring.

Emissaries of loving kindness, that's a fitting descriptor for my nurses. They were all kind and unwaveringly devoted to their vocation. Aman's behavior exemplified my nurses' way of being. He cleaned up after me unhesitatingly. He repositioned me on my bed again and again. He carefully studied the statistics in my EPIC electronic records. He encouraged me repeatedly. Lovingly, he looked me in the eyes and offered his heartening smile.

As Aman was about to depart the hospital at the end of my third day in ICU #22, he offered a cautious word. "I've heard that your docs are considering moving you to the Progressive Care Unit (PCU) on the fourth floor. If they do so, they'll make the move precisely at 6:50 a.m. tomorrow morning. I'm happy for you, but a bit sad for myself. I work again tomorrow here in the ICU. I'll miss you, David. I wish you a speedy recovery."

Unfortunately, a bed was not available in the PCU for another day, so I remained in the ICU, but at least Aman and I were able to get in a few good conversations while I also felt good enough to begin reading former First Lady Michelle Obama's new memoir, *Becoming*.

Sure enough, at exactly 6:50 the following morning, I was transported to the PCU. Arriving in my new room, I was amazed by the absence of all the elaborate technological apparatus I'd gotten used to in the ICU. However, I quickly realized there was an actual window with a view. Room 468 looked out and down towards a beautiful garden. Two new RNs eagerly awaited my arrival.

Kelsey and Lindsay guided my eyes towards the emergency call button, the bed adjustment control, and, with a twinkle in their eyes, the bathroom! Yes, for the first time since being admitted to the hospital, these nurses were encouraging me to take some steps away from the bed and use an actual bathroom.

Still, I didn't roam around much on my first day in the PCU. I was weak and still weary. I was exhausted from all of the in-the-moment "injuries" I had endured for the eventual long term good of my body and soul. I appreciated the necessity of all painful procedures, but I was thoroughly depleted by the process.

It wasn't until my second day in the Progressive Care Unit that I was able to consider a minuscule bit of exploration beyond my room. In the very early dawn hours of (what I would later call) revival morning, nurse Jenni popped into my room and inquired, "Hey there, David, want to start your day by taking a walk around the PCU with me? I'm ready for some sightseeing, are you?"

Jenni looked me right in the eye, like my very best friend, almost daring me with raised eyebrows, to take her arm. Much to my surprise, her direct and playful manner instigated my response, "Well, yes I am." Before you knew it, I was alert, standing tall, and requesting Jenni to make sure that my hospital gown was properly tied in the back so that I wouldn't embarrass myself out there "in the world." And we were off.

Over the next two days, Jenni and her assistant, Debby, coaxed and wheedled me into a distinctly different pattern of patient behavior. They activated me. They got me up and around. They reached into me and lifted me out of the touch-and-go state I'd been in just forty-eight hours before and positioned me in a strikingly different space—a place of hope and encouragement.

Debby and Jenni reintroduced me to life, and living.

I departed the hospital on New Year's Day. As Karen drove me home, I reminisced about the adventure I'd just experienced. I'd been re-introduced to one of the most compassionate communities I'd ever known, Legacy Good Samaritan Hospital. A truly superb interventional radiologist, Kevin Semonsen, MD, an artist and wizard, had attended to me. I'd come to truly admire and respect my highly skilled team of physicians: Brandon Young, Jeffrey Buehler, Meghan Nesmith, and Karen Weis, PCU internist. I'd been encircled with loving kindness and expertise from all the nurses and their assistants. And Karen and I had become even more lovingly intertwined.

Much to my surprise, my hospital adventure has also become a messenger of encouragement. A hospital episode that could have turned out to be deeply discouraging has turned into a wonderfully encouraging experience. I now want to share the encouragement I've received from my health care team, which engulfed me with their superb technical know-how, but even more so, bestowed upon me much-needed inspiration in an extremely difficult time. By sharing this story, I hope to live into what E.B. White, author of the beloved classic, *Charlotte's Web*, might have meant when he said, "The writer's duty is to lift people up, not lower them down."

Over the years, when challenges have appeared at my doorstep, messengers of encouragement have always also appeared. I take to heart the words of Rumi, the thirteenth century Persian poet:

"Be grateful for whoever comes,

because each has been sent as a guide from beyond."

After I've weathered and sorted through the raw emotions of storms such as the one in this story, I try to look with gratitude for guidance from it. Sometimes that takes me quite a while! Having experienced such medical challenges and other of life's difficulties and disappointments over the decades, I've come to trust and even gently expect that I will eventually be guided toward an opportunity. The opportunity is always some paradoxical form of both returning to my true self and starting anew.

Like Robert Duvall in the film *Tender Mercies*, one of my all-time favorites, I too was down and out during this health crisis. My luck had turned south, although through no fault of my own. This film shows and reflects on the ways the former country-western singer Duvall plays eventually regains his strength, literally and spiritually, and in the process he begins a fresh life. Tenderly, Tess Harper, playing Rosa Lee, encourages him through her own support and her helpful challenges of him. In my own story, Rosa Lee was played by many nurses, assistants, and my wife, Karen.

While navigating life's seas, I unexpectedly found myself blessed by the storm that came out of the blue. Battered, my "boat" was rescued and patched up by wholehearted, compassionate and gifted folks. I'm now repainting my boat and making sure its name, *The Encourager*, can be seen easily. In this spirit, I'm looking forward to my 85th birthday in the coming months.

My Physician Is A Dinosaur

An exceptional relationship between a physician and patient brings well-being to both.

Until recently, Paul Hull, M.D., was my primary care doctor for a couple of decades. He was an internist and a messenger of encouragement. He worked in a clinic where some patients require a language translator and where many patients might describe themselves as having limited financial means. Dr. Hull enthusiastically served those who are both able-bodied and those who are experiencing serious debilitating conditions.

His physician friends, who are also still members of my health care team, called him a "dinosaur," an obvious term of endearment. My cardiologist considered Paul Hull to be a dinosaur because "he was a medical practitioner out of a bygone era, a physician who cared for patients as they deserve to be cared for." She added, "Paul took whatever time was needed to build a long-term relationship with each and every one of his patients. He was a physician's physician. He exemplified what's best about medical practice." Every other physician who knew and associated with Dr. Hull described him in a similar fashion. They respected and admired him; they revered him. They even said that Dr. Hull's way of doctoring encouraged them to be more patient-oriented.

Before he retired, and on his day off, Dr. Hull and I met for a conversation about his work. He said, "I love being a primary care doc. The pay is less than what most specialists receive. However, it's the niche in the medical world where the patient-physician relationship is paramount. Relationship building is all there is, you know. If I weren't completely knowledgeable about each one of my patients, have a thorough appreciation of my specialist physician colleagues, and know how to match my patients with specialists, I'd need to leave the work. Technical knowledge is not enough. Expertise takes you only so far. I'm a primary care physician because that's the role that allows me to most deeply know and care for my patients."

Dr. Hull spoke about a certain kind of relationship with his patients, one that, as a friend and colleague said, is built on inclusiveness and imagines a connection with them over time. Rather than merely a relationship built on specialized technical expertise, which clearly he valued in his colleagues, he wanted to know his patients as individual people. So, in addition to his deep knowledge about my particular health conditions, Dr. Hull's broader knowledge of who I am as a person allowed him to make good matches for me to the specialists I've needed.

Significantly, Dr. Hull told me in a variety of ways that he believed in me and regularly included me in decisions about my care. For instance, he told me I know my body well and he trusted in my capacity to make wise decisions about my health care. When there was a particular decision to be made or when we were discussing an approach to optimum well-being, Dr. Hull included a variety of perspectives and possibilities in our conversation: relevant information from my own health history, what he understood from the medical research literature, his observations of the experiences of other patients in similar situations, and his own personal narrative, if appropriate. Then he'd ask, "So, all these things considered, what do you think? What might be the right path for you to take?" By sharing information from several types of sources and asking me this question, he motivated me to actively engage in the decision and to reach into my own wisdom. I felt encouraged to believe that I had some knowledge about myself, that I could figure things out. Thus, he offered me his confidence that I could believe in myself. I was encouraged to be an active partner in my health care.

Both the fact of our similar ages and the fact that Dr. Hull sometimes talked about his own health challenges and how he'd dealt with them more fully humanized my relationship with him. His openness encouraged me to believe my own challenges were surmountable and I too could overcome or live with, if necessary, my personal conditions.

Dr. Hull also offered me encouragement in the way he managed to figure out how to negotiate new dimensions of health care. Having a doctor who was proactive in challenging situations at the system level made me believe he would also find a way to sort out challenging individual health situations for me. For instance, when I asked Dr. Hull about his apprehensions concerning the health care system, he shared a myriad of his personal experiences over the years with insurance carriers and hospitals as organizations. "For me," he explained, "they've often been hurdles to overcome. They've been the way of the world that has forced me to use every bit of my ingenuity to make things work for my patients and me. They have been the major challenges to my vocation." And then he confessed, "But EPIC, our medical data recording system, has been my undoing. Having to find just the right tiny category to describe my patient's condition is challenging and time-consuming. If I were to write my life's memoir, it would have this title: *A Geezer Crawls Up Mt. EPIC.*" Dr. Hull admitted, "As an old guy new to recording health data in the ways of the computer, I need a lot of help." For a physician who was all about relating to people and the complexity of medical situations, the system requirement to break down and categorize his perceptions into multiple check-off boxes didn't capture the intricacies of the human condition. The EPIC system did allow him to write a narrative, and I suspect his narratives were quite lengthy. I'm grateful he wanted to record a complete picture of me so others would have a fuller sense of my health and how to work with me as a person.

When asked about his thoughts regarding the future of health care and medical practice, Paul Hull beamed. "The best is yet to come...I am so impressed with the young people who are entering medical practice right now. The new docs who've come into our clinic are such good physicians. I'm so fortunate to know Dr. Anne Weinsoft and to watch her interact with her colleagues and her patients. New physicians like her give me hope."

That he felt so encouraged by the young docs encouraged me about the future of medicine. Despite the fact that so many new doctors leave the profession early on, combined with the stories of complaints about the health care system from both the public and the medical profession, Dr. Hull's capacity to see with a positive perspective in the face of negative conditions encouraged me to believe in the physicians I'll be working with in the future; I'm going to continue to get great care. He gave me faith and great hope regarding how I will be cared for and how others will be too.

I've been so lucky to have Paul Hull, M.D. on board with me. Even though retired, he continues to encourage me with his positive attitude and his contagious hope for the future. I recently received an invitation from him that might encourage both our continuing relationship and foster ongoing conversations about the power of patient-physician relationships in medical practice. He wants me to join him to co-author a piece on the major benefits of strong and meaningful physician-patient relationships. Of course, I accepted his invitation.

And so, Dr. Hull's dinosaur ways will be amplified. And, perhaps our physician-patient relationship might turn toward a friendship between two older men who both want to encourage others.

ALASKAN TREASURES

Honor the People

The Ice Rink Lesson

The Night the Northern Lights Blessed Our Home

The Bus Driver's Gift

"Gentle Man, Be with Us"

Getting Out of My Brain

Walking Them Home

Honor the People

Encounters with Alaska Native peoples encourage me to live and lead with humility.

While I lived in Alaska, I participated in a project that sought to better understand Alaskan village schools that "worked." These schools served small, isolated, rural communities off the road system, with access typically only by small plane or boat. The mostly K-12 schools provided learning opportunities that made a difference in the lives of the youth and the community.

Typically, early on a Monday morning, I would climb aboard a yellow four-seater Tyee Airlines prop (propeller) plane, sometimes a float- or ski-plane, and I would journey out to a remote school site deep in the central interior of the state, on the edge near the Bering Sea, or to an island location in Southeast Alaska. Usually staying several days and overnighting in local homes or in the school, I observed in classrooms and talked with teachers, took notes about promising practices, attended the local governing school committee meeting and spoke with its members, and joined in school and community cultural events, listening to and talking with anyone I could. The work was challenging, productive, and extremely interesting. In all, what we learned about village schools that "worked" encouraged positive statewide conversations about school reform, and I was pleased to have been a part of this initiative.

But quite aside from the educational results that accrued, I believe that the time I spent in the villages of rural Alaska made it possible for me to learn how to "honor the people." Through their honesty and openness, the Native peoples I encountered in Alaska taught me how to honor them and others by listening deeply, maintaining calm quiet, and acting with humility.

"When you feel full of yourself with wise thoughts," my friend William, himself an Alaska Native, suggested, "that is precisely the time you must maintain silence. We don't need you to tell us all that you know; that's for the rest of us to discover about you, in due time. To know you, we don't need you to talk. Your job is to listen, and to listen deeply. Please listen with your heart."

In another Alaska Native community Peter, a village elder, extended this lesson, thereby helping me understand humility as a way of being that makes it possible to honor people. As Peter prepared to facilitate a village council meeting where I was to bring "Greetings from the State," he whispered, "Just remember, David, it's all about honoring these people, these people at the table. They don't want to hear any pontification. They don't believe in gurus. They don't care about movie stars. They won't consider you an important person. The State of Alaska doesn't mean that much to them. They don't appreciate speeches. You can ask them questions—provided the questions are honest and sincere. They value trust and deep listening. That's it, that's all. What they want from a leader is to be honored."

Some years later, I wrote a poem entitled "Honor the People"© that speaks to both what I learned and how I endeavor to be.

Here is its beginning:

> Honor the people; it's the leader's work.
> Honor them with honest questioning,
> inviting their surprises, believing in their truth.
>
> Honor the people by deeply listening,
> always trusting in what they know.
>
> Listen for their cries.
> Listen for their passions.
> Listen for what the people know.

I believe who and how I am today was encouraged by the Native peoples I encountered in the villages of Alaska. Ever since those yellow prop plane days, seven words have offered constant direction to my life: "Honor the people; it's the leader's work." Since then, in both professional settings such as in the college classes I taught and the schools I led, and in personal relationships, such as within the family I love and the friendships I've been given, I've endeavored to earnestly practice listening deeply, maintaining calm quiet, and acting with humility, all as paths toward honoring the people. I am ever grateful for such encouragement by the Alaska Native peoples I met.

The Ice Rink Lesson

A father and son encourage me to listen for others' passions.

Wintertime in Fairbanks, Alaska, came with its challenges. Typical January temperatures hovered in the neighborhood of twenty below zero. Some of my jogging friends would brave the cold and continue their pastime outdoors. I chose an alternative venue; my wintertime five-mile course was a narrow track circling the Olympic-size hockey rink at the University of Alaska Fairbanks.

When the hockey team was practicing, my run was energized as I watched the puck careening at lightning speed back and forth across the rink. When the team was away, I still used the track for my fitness routine. And, on one occasion, such a quieter time presented me with a lesson that significantly changed my life.

Late one afternoon, I noticed a university colleague and his eight-year old son in the very middle of the immense rink. My friend, Peter, was teaching his son, Andrew, how to ice skate. He was helping Andrew keep his knees bent and his chest up as he glided along. As I circumnavigated the rink time and time again, I noticed Peter's calm and patient teaching style.

At the conclusion of my exercise session, while Andrew was in the locker room, I said to Peter, "I was so impressed with your way of being with Andrew out there on the ice. What's your secret, Peter?"

"Andrew's a kid who's always struggled," Peter said, "in school and at home. So, early on, I just focused on what Andrew seemed to have a zeal for. Ever since he learned to walk, Andrew has been totally enthralled with hockey and skates. It's his major delight. We attend all the university home games. And so, I'm trying my very best to help Andrew learn to ice skate. For some time now my motto has been, 'Find out what he's passionate about, then pour it on.'"

Although born naturally positive, even optimistic, I'd not given much active thought to the practice of thoughtful encouragement. In subsequent conversations, Peter and I talked a good bit about what caring encouragement requires. Such encouragement entails attentive and meticulous observation in the moment, a steady sense of inconspicuous watchfulness over time, the asking of honest questions and deep listening throughout. That's what Peter and I came to believe. I believe it now, more strongly than ever.

These days my thoughtful encouragement practice remains primarily focused on family, friends, and colleagues. And, over time I've come to understand that this way of being with them is not always easy and straightforward. For instance, what's to be my response to a person who constantly belittles other people in an effort to always be right or in control? During a recent social occasion, I observed a fellow finding fault with each and every comment made by another person in the room. Toward the end of the evening, the fault-finder approached me, looking me right in the eye. I had watched for this opportunity all evening. I asked him, "What are you yearning for in your life, John?"

After a period of silence, he put his hand over his heart and offered a watery-eyed response, "I just want to find a small piece of land where I can live out my life in peace and quiet. I'm not much good with people, but I'm okay on my own." At that point, we were interrupted and he closed the conversation with, "Thanks, David, for listening and encouraging me."

Find out what they're passionate about, then pour it on. It's been thirty years since I first heard that jewel of wise instruction. I don't know whether Andrew has gone on to be a hockey star. But I do know that I've learned to be a better encourager.

The Night The Northern Lights Blessed Our Home

Community help and nocturnal enchantment welcome us into our new lives.

The house at 1350 Viewpointe Drive in Fairbanks, Alaska, was ordinary in one sense; it was a tract home. But it was the first home Karen, my wife, and I owned together. And, it was far from ordinary in yet another sense. It was set high on a hill just north of town and looked out on the Alaska Range, including the mountain that the Athabaskan and other Alaska Native peoples call "the Great One, Denali."

Situated above the ice fog in winter, we looked out on clear skies during the few mid-winter daylight hours. In the summer, we were able to do all of the gardening we desired in a series of terraces that cascaded down to the street. The extra hours of summer light in the land of the Midnight Sun gave our garden a big boost.

Our lives in Fairbanks were blessed from the start. At the time, I was the principal of Denali Elementary, having started in that position a couple of months earlier. I already knew from my initial experience that the students, teachers, parents, and neighbors associated with that school were special. However, on the day we moved into our new home, I learned just how special.

We made the move in late October, which in Fairbanks made it early winter. Luckily, the snow wasn't too deep at that time, so for the most part, the physical logistics of loading and hauling all our material possessions wasn't as difficult as it could have been. Twenty teachers and parents showed up to lend a hand. All day, they ferried furniture and clothing in their packed pick-up trucks and overloaded cars from the house we'd been renting to our own new home. Once the final truckload of goods had arrived and been located in the designated rooms, all the parents and teachers gathered in the kitchen and placed a generous and delicious potluck dinner out for all of us to enjoy together.

Their huge contribution of energy, goodwill, and spirit encouraged us. We didn't have to pay for movers; at the end of the day everything was in its new rightful place. But more significantly, we'd gotten to know people as people, not just as teachers, not just as parents, but more like we would know neighbors and friends. We experienced the gift of community and a sense of belonging.

But the best was yet to come. One of our school's Alaska Native teachers, Kathleen, told us to grab our caps and jackets and scurry outside. As we gathered in the cold and dark in the front yard, Kathleen directed our attention upward and told us, "Look up! The auroras are showering a blessing."

We were spellbound. The northern lights were even more magnificent than usual. The greens and pinks and the glowing whites dazzled. We all watched in awe. But what was most unusual was the direction that the auroras were traveling.

Ordinarily, we saw them in intermittent horizontal waves, high in the sky or toward the horizon. On this night, we watched aurora showers. As the northern lights rained down upon us, Kathleen gave a call: "The spirits are blessing this home for David and Karen!" She went on to whisper, "If we're real quiet, we'll be able to hear the auroras."

Well, I believe that our Alaska Native parents and teachers were the only ones to actually hear the northern lights. I'd long felt that Alaska Native ways of knowing are far better developed than are mine.

As our school friends departed later that evening, they shared these words with us: "The spirits wish to give you heart and give you peace."

Even thirty years later, this encouraging experience resides in my heart and memory as one of the most significant of my life. It increased my confidence in a bright future for us as a couple and for the school community of which I was now a part.

The Bus Driver's Gift

During a difficult transition, encouragement comes from a very unexpected source, and community connectedness supports a newcomer.

1983 was a tough year for me.

Besides a significant health scare, the main challenge was to my parenting responsibilities. I was a newly single parent, and it was my inability to prepare good meals for my teenage son that almost did me in.

My teenage son, Bruce, and I lived in a small cabin on North Douglas Island, across the bridge and way to the north of downtown Juneau, Alaska, a new town for us.

The school bus didn't come anywhere near where we lived. So, Bruce took our truck each morning. I walked a mile each day to take the Juneau city bus at the end of its line to the University of Alaska Southeast where I was a college professor. I rode back home on the bus each night.

When I arrived home, my immediate concern was supper. I'd never enjoyed cooking, nor did I have much practice at it. Preparing delicious meals for the two of us was not my strong suit. But I tried my best. I scoured magazines at the supermarket and bought a cookbook or two. At work, I'd ask my friends for good cooking ideas.

I thought that I was preparing pretty decent meals. But to hear Bruce talk, that was definitely not the case. After hauling water and cranking up the cook stove, I'd place a meal in front of Bruce. Often his reaction was, "Not this again, Dad!"

So, I was at my wit's end regarding feeding the boy. One day, as I rode the bus back home, I was in a hopeless, teary condition.

As the last rider to be dropped off, I sat just across the aisle and slightly behind the driver, Frank. He leaned toward me and said, "Tough day at the office, David?"

"No, Frank, many tough days at the stove." And then I told him the whole gory story. Not only did I tell Frank about how my meals didn't seem to satisfy my son, but also that I felt quite troubled that this one time of the day Bruce and I had together was being negatively impacted. Actually, I was concerned for our father-son relationship. Frank listened carefully.

Then he pulled the bus over to the side of the road. We were near the end of the line. Frank got out a little notebook and wrote a recipe for potato, vegetable, and ground beef casserole. I was really surprised and grateful for his unexpected generosity.

"Thanks, Frank."

As I walked the last mile home, I felt the most encouraged I'd been in weeks!

About a week later, while having lunch in the faculty dining hall, I was called to the front of the room. Other folks put down their forks and turned their attention toward me and the dean of our small faculty, who presented me with a notebook. Initially, I only noticed the word "lifesaving" on the cover. "What's going on?" I asked.

Looking inside, I discovered suppertime recipes autographed by all fourteen of the men and women in our department. I was simply astonished!

"Whose idea was this? "I asked.

Everyone called back the response in unison, "Bus 12's driver, Frank."

I found out later that when Frank got home the night he shared his casserole recipe, he called our faculty secretary, Molly, and suggested all of my colleagues in the Education Department take up a collection of simple and easy recipes for me.

Frank reportedly told Molly, "You could place those recipes in a binder with this title on the cover: *Lifesaving Recipes for David.*"

The recipes did save my life! Far fewer supper-time complaints arrived with the various concoctions that my friends taught me how to prepare. As the year went on, the quality of our meals improved significantly. Our father-son relationship became better and better as well. And for sure, there were no more tears shed by me on Capital Transit Systems bus number 12. Thanks, Frank.

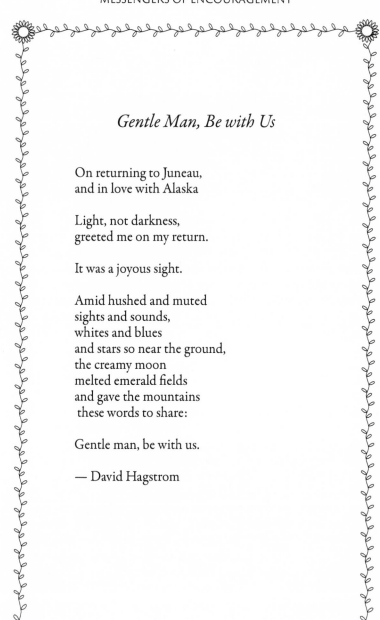

Gentle Man, Be with Us

On returning to Juneau,
and in love with Alaska

Light, not darkness,
greeted me on my return.

It was a joyous sight.

Amid hushed and muted
sights and sounds,
whites and blues
and stars so near the ground,
the creamy moon
melted emerald fields
and gave the mountains
 these words to share:

Gentle man, be with us.

— David Hagstrom

Getting Out of My Brain

A new poet friend coaxes me into a different way of approaching leadership.

The best advice I ever received about being a leader came while on a walk with William Stafford—for many years, the Poet Laureate of Oregon—through Totem Park in Sitka, Alaska. We were both attending the Sitka Writing Symposium. As we began to get to know one another, meeting daily for an early morning walk or run and talking about our writing efforts, Bill asked me questions such as, "What's it like for you to be an elementary school principal?" He seemed to encourage my sharing, so I decided to enlist his aid in thinking out an issue that was troubling me. Having been recently appointed to lead a school I wasn't acquainted with in Fairbanks, I was in a fog about how to more deeply engage the community within and surrounding the school. I had used up all of what I'd learned during my days in graduate school, and even what I'd taught my own graduate students about more current thinking, and felt that I did not any longer have a clue as to how to make a difference in my school for the children, for the teachers, for the community, or for myself. I was stalled.

Bill Stafford listened to me patiently on loop after loop throughout the beautiful park. And then, in front of a particularly striking Alaska Native totem pole, he stopped and looked me straight in the eye and asked with a quietness that feels soft and easy even as I remember it today, "David, I think you're stuck in your brain. You're trying to grind out an answer. That'll never work. Go to sleep tonight asking these questions, 'Who are these people you're with? And, what are they calling for?' Tomorrow morning, when we're on our walk, tell me your answers." Given that it wasn't working for me to think out an approach and because I felt desperate, I figured I might was well try his alternative.

Every morning over that next week, I responded to Bill's "Who are these people?" and "What are they calling for?" questions. I talked about how lots of people really didn't want to be in Fairbanks, where they found themselves because of circumstances rather than choice. For example, there were the military personnel and their families for whom interior Alaska wasn't their desired assignment or the Alaska Native people, whose lack of "cash work" in their villages brought them into town to find such work. I talked about all the clever ways some of the more well-to-do-parents tried to smuggle their children out of our school to what they thought were better schools. Each day, William Stafford listened and he smiled and said, "I believe you're getting somewhere, David. Let's keep on talking about this tomorrow."

I did keep talking with Bill, but the big turnaround came when I was back at school. With the "Who are these people?" and "What are they calling for?" inquiries still in the back of my mind, I asked questions of every one of the adult family members and neighbors I met. I found myself wanting to know everything about them. "How did they find themselves here in this Fairbanks neighborhood? What did they like best about it? What was their impression of the school?" And what turned out to be a million dollar question, "If you weren't talking with me at this moment, what would you rather be doing?" Fortunately, this question simply came to me one day as a concrete way to indirectly urge someone to talk about who they were as a person, rather than only speaking about themselves in relation to their roles. That question usually led to: "What are the most creative things you do in your life?" And, then, "Would you be willing to do some of your creative work here in our school?

I asked these questions out of my desire to get to know, especially, the parent makeup of my new school community and simply because I'm inherently interested in whoever happens to cross my path. I was also interested in strengthening families' and the neighborhood's connections with our school and increasing our resources. The parents responded to my questions eagerly, even gratefully it seemed, saying they hadn't been asked before about themselves and their perspectives. I got the impression they wanted to be recognized and heard. Perhaps this was, at a deep level, what they were calling for.

Over time, the creative contributions of families and neighbors helped to bring the school alive and encouraged the development of our school community. Those with horticultural interests initiated work on a community garden. Those with experiences in hiking and exploring Alaska's backcountry established a winter survival course for the children. Alaska Native elders, who profoundly understood astronomy, offered opportunities for night-time observing and hearing traditional oral stories about the heavens. Artists began to bring their talent into the school. One particularly ingenious artist created, with the help of the children, a large stained glass remembrance of the neighborhood's history, which was installed above the entrance to the school. With their assistance, our school became a community bursting with productive activity. Each fruitful endeavor encouraged us to be even more inclusive and invitational of others and to try something else new.

As a school leader in Fairbanks, my holding of William Stafford's inquiries and the specific ways I discovered to invite families' and neighbors' genuine responses quieted my unproductive efforts to solve problems on my own and opened up creative, and often surprising, possibilities for the school community. Thus, Bill Stafford encouraged me into a new way of being, a new way of engaging, and a new way of listening. I was then able to encourage others to offer their creativity and hard work on behalf of the school and its children.

It's been years since those walks with Bill through Sitka's Totem Park and my work as an elementary school principal, yet I find myself returning to his inquiries when I'm with a new group and now, too, when meeting a new person. Yes, knowing "Who are these people?" and "What are they calling for?"

intrigues me. But more importantly, learning what they have to share in response helps me know how I might best encourage them to be most fully who they are and to offer their special gifts to the world.

Walking Them Home

An Alaska Native teacher encourages me and together, she and I encourage greater family involvement in our school.

As an elementary school principal in Fairbanks, Alaska, I was puzzled about the absence of Alaska Native parents in the ongoing life of our school community. The Alaska Native children were always present; they made up one-third of our school population. But, where were their parents, guardians, and extended family members? I never noticed them at school events and they did not often attend teacher-parent conferences; in fact, I rarely observed them bringing their children to school.

So, a couple of months into my work at the school, I approached one of the Alaska Native teachers, Kathleen, with whom I felt I had a very positive relationship, and asked if she would be willing to help me understand the situation. She explained the absence of the parents in this way: Many of these parents attended school themselves in the villages far from Alaska's major cities. Often they had very difficult experiences in those rural schools. In many of the village schools in years past, the goal of the non-Native educators had been to replace a Native Alaskan language with English. Teachers thought that if the children were proficient in English, they would be better prepared for their later encounters in the wider world. They may not have realized that language carries culture and in being a part of diminishing a Native language, they were also a part of diminishing Native ways of life. Or they may have actively wanted their students to assimilate into what they saw as the dominant white culture. Those teachers' efforts were often met with unhappiness and anger. The teachers often alienated the village community and made life difficult for the children and their families. Kathleen concluded, "Many of the parents of the children we serve, they just hated school. Their memories of school are extremely unpleasant. They just want to stay away."

I asked Kathleen, "How are we going to encourage the parents to become a part of our school community?"

Kathleen said, "David, you're just going to have to walk them home. And, as you do so, you will need to carefully listen along the way."

"How do I do that?" I asked, equally as puzzled by her solution as I initially had been by the parents' absence. "How do I walk the parents into the school?" Kathleen suggested that on the next morning I find my way out to a street corner approximately six blocks from our school building and observe.

The next morning I told Kathleen I found a couple dozen Alaska Native parents out there six blocks away, saying goodbye to their children and sending them our way.

She nodded. "Six blocks is their safety place. That's just about as close to any school that they'd like to come." She told me to return to the same location the next morning and to begin to invite them towards the school. "It'll be very difficult work, and it will take a good bit of time but your presence, rather than your words, will encourage the beginning of trust within the parent community." She believed that my being present day after day with these family members would, sooner or later, foster a sense that our school could be their school home too.

The next morning I was out there meeting some of our Alaska Native parents, six blocks from the school building. Quietly, I said, "Good morning, I'm David Hagstrom. I'm the principal at Denali School." I was met with very little talk. Nor did I say more.

I began this endeavor to involve Alaska Native parents and families more fully in the life of the school beginning in early October. By the middle of that month the group had only moved about a half a block. Over the coming weeks, we steadily but slowly traveled toward the school building.

Taking Kathleen's advice, I listened very carefully as the

parents pointed to house after house, volunteering about their own children that "Brenda lives here. Peter lives there." As we walked, I not only learned who lived where, but also heard stories of relocation from their familial villages into the urban center of Fairbanks. I learned about the talents and gifts of my new company of walkers. "Nathan knows how to tell direction by the stars." "Oscar understands the best ways to ensure our safety and survival in the wintertime." "Angela knows how to tan a moose skin."

I was beginning to feel we were becoming like friends. Sarah one day declared *hoozoonh ts'e neel'ekk'o naanuhletoyh*, translating those Tanana tribal words for me, "We were beginning to care for each other." That described my feelings precisely.

On a mid-December morning, about ten weeks after our journey first began, twenty-five Alaska Native parents and I entered Denali School. Kathleen, my mentor in this endeavor, met us at the door and gave us all cookies and hot chocolate. She greeted the parents in this way, "Welcome to your new school home. We're so pleased you're here. This is going to be a good place for you, just as it is for your children."

Over the next couple of years, most Alaska Native parents and guardians became regulars within the school. They began to drop off and pick up their children, stepping inside the school to do so. Some joined in the activities of the parent association, others helped in the school garden, especially during the summer when the crops needed attention during the swift growing season. They began to attend parent conferences. Initially, all our steps toward inclusion were smaller ones. But eventually, we dedicated a wing of the building to Alaska Native education. Native elders taught all the children astronomy, winter survival skills, Alaska Native stories, and so much more. Looking back on the six-block journey of walking and listening, the effort brought our school community closer together and improved the curriculum for children—benefits that could never, ever have been imagined.

Kathleen's suggestion that I "walk them home" evolved into a far more significant and inclusive way of being within our school community. It became important that we all truly knew and appreciated one another. Over time, we became more of a genuine community. And I learned that "community" is a gift that is received, rather than achieved, through being truly present to one another.

GIFTS OF TRAVEL

"Traveling"

What Do You Do for Your Living?

How Is Your Spirit Today?

Life Is Beautiful

Chemin Du Coeur

En Silencio Florece el Alma

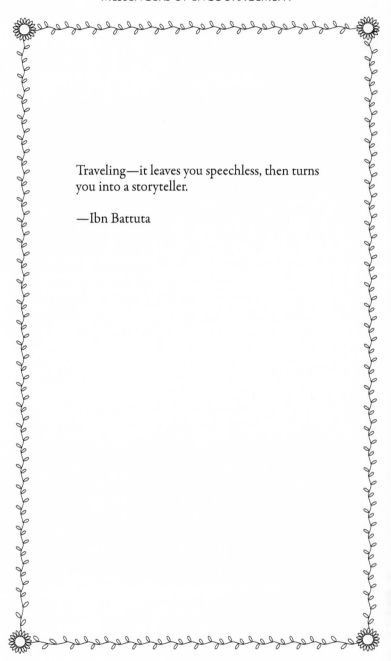

Traveling—it leaves you speechless, then turns you into a storyteller.

—Ibn Battuta

What Do You Do for Your Living?

A grape harvesting manager sets me on a quest to discover my true heart.

In early September 2000, my wife, Karen, and I arrived at a farmhouse in the Var department of Provence, France, where we planned to spend two months during our semester-long university sabbaticals. The farmhouse, set in the center of vineyards, was shuttered up tight. I enjoyed opening up the doors and windows, inviting the light into this simply renovated nineteenth-century abode. I was recovering from heart surgery and Jeff and Tessa, the owners, had offered to loan us their property. In fact, Jeff as my physician, even wrote me a prescription for "six weeks in Provence!" Tessa had promised the farmhouse was charming and magical.

About a week after our settling in, *les vendages*, the grape harvest, started up in full swing. As I watched the industrious undertaking just outside our windows, I recalled Jeff's parting words once we'd accepted his and Tessa's invitation, "They'll be harvesting the grapes when you're there. You should have a fascinating time." Knowing of my interest in writing, he volunteered, "You could be harvesting your life stories inside the house while they're harvesting grapes just outside the door."

It was a spellbinding experience observing *les vendanges*. I watched the grapes being picked by hand and also by a gargantuan French-blue harvesting machine. The process went on for days. And for days, I sat in a chair at the edge of the field, totally engaged and enthralled.

The person in charge of *les vendanges* was a fellow named Albert. Jeff thought I'd be captivated by him. So, I watched

Albert carefully.

Day after day, I looked his way. Finally, I got up the courage to ask to take a photo of Albert. Given my extremely limited French, I gestured at my camera and then towards him. "Photo, Albert? Photo okay, Albert?" When he noticed me, Albert was smiling broadly.

"Of course you may take my picture, David. Do you want me out among the vines, or up on my machine?"

Stunned by his facility with English and his using my name, I blurted out, "Oh, up on the machine. But how is it that you know my name?"

"Oh, I know all about you."

Albert leaned out of the machine and as I shook his offered hand, he continued, "What do you do for your living?" That being a typical question for introducing oneself in the United States, but, as it turns out, not in France. I told him I was a college professor, and he said, "Oh, I didn't mean how you get your paycheck, I want to know how you live."

Speechless, I just stood there for what felt like the longest time. I wasn't at all sure what he was asking.

Finally, given my silence, he said, "Have you selected your *santon*?"

Santon? "Well, uh no. What is a *santon*?"

Albert explained that all across France people collect these little ceramic painted Provençal figures that represent various occupations. So *santons* embody the roles played in a village such as baker, priest, mayor, shopkeeper, even fool. Customarily, they are placed next to the *crèche* or manger at Christmas time declaring the wide range of persons who've come to celebrate the birth of baby Jesus.

"But, here in our community, we also make use of *santons* in a different way." Albert stepped down from the big blue machine, walked closer to me and said, "My friends and I use *santons* as a personal metaphor for the way we live our lives."

We sat down next to each other on the ground and Albert resumed, "*Santons* represent who we are in our hearts. Do you know what I mean, David?"

I did understand.

Albert pointed to the southwest and suggested I go to the city of Nice and look around the shops there for my very own *santon*. Along the side streets, he promised I'd find a number of shops that carry the little figures. Albert advised me to carefully choose one. "Remember, David, the question I asked you was, 'What do you do for your living? How do you live your life?'"

Early the next week, Karen and I drove to Nice and I checked out the shops. Since I typically don't like shopping, Karen was amazed I spent so much time going from store to store. I was truly on a mission and a rather challenging one at that. *Who am I really, in my heart? What do I truly do for my living? And, how do I live?*

These were such complex questions, such daunting issues. I looked and looked, and looked some more, at these statuettes. I saw one of a gardener and thought, maybe this is the one for me. I've always felt called to "make desert places green," to recover land that needed re-invigorating or to develop spaces to bring out their natural beauty. Both at our family farm in Wisconsin and, later, at our cabin in Oregon, I've tried to listen to the land, and make of these places strikingly pleasing and thriving spaces. Professionally, I'd always been drawn to the difficult and challenging assignments that needed tending. So, maybe, the gardener *santon*?

And then, my gaze fell upon a smiling fellow who was holding a lantern in his left hand and an umbrella on his right arm. I stood before him, riveted. *Are you, me? Am I, you? Are you the metaphor that represents my heart? Is this my way of living?*

It helped that he was carrying an umbrella. We do that a lot in Portland, Oregon. I remembered times I'd shared my umbrella with passers-by on the street. Also, it seemed with his kind smile that he was the encouraging type. I'd spent a lifetime figuring out quiet ways to encourage friends and family members.

And, surely, this *santon* that seized hold of me would brighten up the dark night for others, perhaps doing so without a spoken word. He looked so willing to reassure.

In my experience, simply putting a little light on an issue or problem and listening attentively was much more appropriate than preaching, moralizing, or advising. For me, the lantern represented difficulties well lit, understood, and prepared for solution.

I purchased the lantern-holding, umbrella-carrying, kind-looking *santon*. I brought him back to the farmhouse and held him up for Albert to see. I wanted him to know that I'd found my *santon*, that it accurately depicted my way of life. As Albert made the turn onto another row of vines, he brought his gigantic blue harvesting machine to a full stop. He gave me a thumbs-up, and called out, "Good work, David! Your *santon* will remind you of who you are during your stay here and when you return home."

In the days that followed, I kept my *santon* on a small table that served as my writing desk in the farmhouse, the place that, as had been predicted, I harvested my life stories. I'd write a paragraph and then glance at my lantern-holding, umbrella-carrying, kind-looking *santon*. This fellow had come into my life to encourage me, as had Albert. To this day, my *santon* sits on my home writing desk.

I still carry those words written on the prescription form, "six weeks in Provence!" and often recall Tessa's description of the farmhouse: "It's a restorative and life-giving home for the heart." Especially, I'm grateful for Albert's generosity as he connected me with the wisdom of the Provençal *santons* with his question, "What do you do for your living?" All these words and my *santon* helped my heart to recover during our stay at the farmhouse and encouraged my spirit in the coming years.

How Is Your Spirit Today?

Genuinely greeting each other proves to be a real challenge.

"How are you?"

As a way of greeting another person those three words don't usually lead to an honest or genuine connection between people. And, as a person who values honest and genuine connections, I want to encourage myself and others to create them.

Of course, whether the literal words "How are you?" bring about or deepen a relationship depends on the situation. Is it the cashier at the grocery store, whom I've never met, asking me "How are you?" Is it a neighbor I often see on my walks around the block? Is it my spouse asking as she looks me right in the eye first thing in the morning? Or, am I asking the question of an office colleague as we quickly pass each other in the hallway? "How are you?" may serve merely as a quick effort at politeness or, depending on its intonation and the intent conveyed with accompanying nonverbals, can be a sincere inquiry of concern and interest.

Often, however, "How are you?" simply replaces the greeting of "hi" or "hello" and gives way to a quick nod by the asker. What's to be said in return? "I'm well, thank you" or "Life is good," even if that is not the way I feel at the moment? It's admittedly easier to say such things, especially when time is brief, and usually it is, and particularly if I don't want to intrude on another's attention or be vulnerable myself.

How can an honest and genuine connection be encouraged as we greet each other? How might such a greeting even turn into an act of encouragement?

Probably the most intriguing greeting I've ever received

occurred while I was out for a walk on a back road in rural France. Four older gents came upon me, tipped their caps and hailed me, "*Bonjour, monsieur bonhomme, qu'est votre esprit aujourd'hui?*" I smiled and tipped my own cap in return. As a person sorely lacking in essential French language skills, most of what was said thoroughly puzzled me. I could only smile in response.

After the four sporty fellows passed by, I took out the small notepad I carried in my back pocket and wrote down what I thought they'd said to me. Then when I visited our small village post office later in the morning, I showed the English-speaking clerk the words. She initially said, "Monsieur, the way you've written this is not at all correct." After some thought, she added, "I do believe they asked you this, 'Hey old fellow, how is your spirit today?'"

She went on, "Yes, I am quite certain, that was their general intent. However, they may have injected a bit more humor into their question. I'm now thinking they might have asked this, 'Hey geezer guy, how is your spirit today?'"

I laughed heartedly and the La Poste worker chuckled along. As the hilarity subsided, I asked her, "So what do you think I should have offered as the proper French response?"

Grinning rather mischievously she said, "*Ça dépend.* How is your spirit today, Monsieur?"

Smiling broadly, I declared, "Well, as a result of my encounter with the gents and your helpful response, my spirit is really good."

The clerk replied, "So, you would truthfully have answered with something like, '*Bon esprit, messieurs. Merci beaucoup.*' (Good spirit, sirs. Thank you very much.) With a serious inquiry like the one you were posed, you always need to tell the truth."

That morning's experience whisked me back to my home in Oregon, and to my yoga teacher in Portland. Cathleen greets each yoga class with, "Good morning my friends. Let's begin class today with this question. 'Do you have love in your life?' I'm not asking: 'Are you in love?' I'm simply asking, 'Do you feel love in your life, this morning?'" I've always appreciated that question! It's a question that's not to be answered flippantly.

Another serious question that gets my attention is the one that's been recently coming to me as I awake: "How might I be at ease throughout the course of this day?" Just like Cathleen's query, this one leads me to an honest place.

Such questions are probably a bit too profound for use as everyday greetings in the street, at the grocery store, or in a business meeting. But, in the right setting and under the right circumstances, these questions might be suitable for an in-depth and authentic conversation.

If "How are you?" remains cursory and circumstances don't lend themselves to questions of spirit, love, and equanimity, what might a person pose in greeting? There are still many options to engage another person in a more meaningful interaction. Some of my favorites are: "What are you most looking forward to today (during your walk, in this meeting, etc.)?" Or, later on: "What was the best part of your day?" And, for a friend I've not seen in a while: "What do you know now that you didn't know when last we met?" My preferred question asked of my wife first thing many days is: "How might I help you move through this new day?" That inquiry seems to connect easily with her and appears to start her day acceptably. Of course, I need to carefully listen to her response and my actions must meet her needs, if at all possible.

Actually, asking any question of any person beyond a superficial "How are you?" requires that I be willing to listen very carefully to the response. I must accept the responsibility to enter into the life space of the person I've encountered. I am obligated to take a sincere interest, possibly ask follow-up questions, and perhaps offer an encouraging word, an indication of my solid support. Over the years, I've come to understand that those who've shared their problems and troubles, as well as their joys and successes, appreciate an authentic and heartening reply such as "I believe in you" or "I'll be cheering for you."

In my experience, everyday words of greeting can be transformed to invite a real human connection. Although we probably will not use the words I was offered by the French gents or make direct reference to the condition of another's spirit, we can, indeed, inquire about their state of mind and heart and encourage each other on our paths.

Life Is Beautiful

In Paris I settle into an eccentric place where everybody knows your name.

At first I did not fall for Le Brio, the café closest to our apartment in Paris. Walking past the place early in my visit, it seemed dumpy and a bit strange. Looking through its large windows, I saw it was decorated with old mismatched wooden furniture, a worn-out red velvet couch with a large stuffed white tiger lounging on it, and a life-size female mannequin wearing a bikini and a boa!

As time went on, I passed the place often on my way to La Poste to buy stamps or to catch the bus, and I found myself peering in those windows, almost offhandedly. If anyone caught me looking in, I'd quickly glance away. However, if the truth were told, Le Brio began to fascinate me. I wasn't so much interested in the story behind the setting; rather, I found myself curious about the people. *Why were the same two older gents always seated in the same adjoining bar seats every day at three o'clock? Why were the same two women seated on the tattered red velvet sofa each morning? And why were there often three motorcycles and several bicycles lined up outside?*

One blustery November day, I made my way through the door and inched myself into the only chair and table available— precisely under the TV, at the end of the jam-packed bar— where I ordered a *café*. I began to look around the place; what first caught my eye were the words on a blackboard above the bar: *Wi-Fi password: lavieestbelle.* (Life is beautiful.) Most people were drinking a beer and engaged with each other while I was alone and most likely the only English speaker in the place.

Nonetheless, the animated scene felt good to me. The famous theme song from the TV show *Cheers*, "Where Everybody Knows Your Name," captured the ambiance at Le Brio exactly.

Over the next few weeks, I passed much more time in this Montmartre café. The bartender-waitperson not only offered me a typical "Bonjour" but surprisingly, he also began to offer me a bowed "Namaste." I felt recognized. Especially important to me, the two older gents started to wave to me with both hands each time I walked past them to my seat nearby. Another time, one even asked my name.

Le Brio felt like a charming "third place" right out of Ray Oldenburg's *The Great Good Place*. In that classic 1989 book, home is the "first place," our workspace or office is the "second place," and common areas where the public gathers, such as coffee shops or churches, are identified as "third places." These common spaces are separate from both home and work; they become the anchors of community life.

Toward the end of my time in Paris, as I entered the café for a fond farewell, I was greeted by the two older gents with a wave. "Bonjour, Monsieur Daveed. *Ça va*?" How's it going? Not knowing whether they'd understand me or not, I replied, "*La vie est belle.*"

People in Le Brio encouraged me to come in out of the cold and to settle in among the regulars. They welcomed me and raised my spirits, which heartened me greatly. Still, it seemed to me that Le Brio was more than a collection of people who regularly acknowledged each other. I had experienced a place that by its very nature encouraged connection. Indeed, there was a spirit to the actual place—a playful, lively, openhearted spirit to Le Brio, which its very name conveyed. This place encouraged my confidence to step out of my ordinary perspective and to step into a world I didn't know. In doing so, my world expanded, even without knowing the language.

Chemin Du Coeur

Small country roads in France lead to a larger way of the heart.

When my wife, Karen, and I lived in France, one of my favorite pastimes took us cruising the little country roads, marked C and D on the Michelin maps we used to guide our travels everywhere. Ideal for bicycles, and pretty near perfect for small cars such as our Peugeot 207, we feared instant catastrophe when we met a large SUV coming our way.

The antithesis of four-lane toll-road *autoroutes*, the C and D roads offered narrow and scenic itineraries with instant curves. Packed with test and fun—and the need to be super alert, laser-beam focused or else—there could be absolutely no multi-tasking on these backcountry byways! Plus, I needed to keep up the pace all the other French drivers required, their being renowned for what I'd call tailgating so they could see as far ahead as possible before making a sharp move to pass. Even with what I experienced as nerve-wracking pressure from other drivers, I loved these roads, such as my favorite D35, for the back and forth, up and down of the constantly moving steering wheel. I loved these roads for the challenge they offered, the demand they required and the excitement they provided.

But what I enjoyed even more was finding out what was just around the next bend. We'd pull through a hairpin curve and I'd exclaim, "Wow, will you look at that!" I sure enjoyed anticipating whatever would appear next through our tiny car's windshield.

At one point, we found ourselves tracing one of the French pilgrimage routes, part of the network of spiritual paths that connect with the Camino de Santiago, the well-known track crossing northern Spain, which brings wayfarers from around the globe. I slowed my driving pace considerably and drove quite carefully when I spotted pilgrims at the edge of the road. I felt magnetically attracted to the sight of these "journey folks" with their backpacks, walking sticks and inviting smiles.

A couple of times, I pulled over to talk with small groups or joined them when they later arrived in the square of a small village where I'd awaited. Interestingly, like me—but for different reasons—they were invigorated and energized by what was "just around the bend." One older gent told me, "The walk is as much about the surprising views around the curve as it is about some far-off goal on the horizon." A woman in her twenties disclosed, "This is a pilgrimage of the heart for many of us. Day in and day out, I feel I'm on this little road that's moving me closer and closer to my heart. I'm trying to find out more about who I am."

The pilgrims shared something else about their journey. They spoke of the gracious gift that made each day do-able and the long journey, possible, achievable: the gift of hospitality, of welcome. A young boy asked me, "Have you seen the shells in the house windows?" I nodded yes, I'd seen the scallop shells (*coquille Saint-Jacques*) in windows, on front doors and gates of fences along the road. He continued, saying, "The seashell is our welcome sign. It invites us in for a great meal and a cozy sleep." The boy's dad told me later, "We rest our bodies and hearts where we find the shells. But even more than telling us we'll be taken good care of, the seashells give us hope. Genuine welcome and overnight hospitality will make new horizons possible in the morning. We'll feel great encouragement for the new day's journey and can look forward to its surprises."

En Silencio Florece el Alma

An innkeeper in Spain encourages me with an invitation to silence.

Once upon a time, I found myself at a very small, remote mountain inn near the southern coast of Spain. At the time, there were no other guests. Nestled up against a majestic national park, the inn, perched high above its whitewashed village, looked outward to the Mediterranean Sea, making it possible to see all the way to Morocco with clear conditions. It was Thanksgiving in the United States.

By day my gaze was taken out to sea. At night the village lights twinkled me to sleep. There was no doubt; it was the prettiest place I'd ever seen. For me, it was heaven.

I told the innkeeper, Claire, I'd found paradise. "Indeed you have," she proclaimed. "It's a paradise for your soul. Once you settle in and settle down, the silence will surround you and you'll be home." Watching me take all this to heart, she leaned close and whispered: "*En silencio florece el alma.*" The soul flourishes in silence. "May the silence bring you home this day. May your soul sing you lullabies tonight."

At that she placed a small guest book securely in my hand. "If you will, before you leave, some words from you, perhaps like these." Her eyes directed me to these poetic words written by John, from Yorkshire: "It's in these hills, and beneath this sky, that I find my voice, and I can sing." Then, my gentle hostess slowly walked away.

Graced with these invitations, I passed my day *en silencio*. As the hours moved on by, I remembered moments when my soul felt full and free: at first light during my writing times at early dawn, on hearing clear words of encouragement, and at moments when laughter rocks my heart. I cherished those times when my soul flourished.

I remembered friends and family far away. I sent gratitudes quietly toward them. I wrapped myself in the hills. I somehow climbed into the sky. At day's end, I found myself singing these words:

> I'll listen with my heart to you, my friend.
> I'll listen with my heart.
> I'll bring my peaceful soul to you, my friend.
> I'll bring my peaceful soul.
>
> It's the gift that's mine to give,
> It's the song that's mine to sing.
> May I pass these words along to you?
> May I give my words to you?

I couldn't be around a table with family and friends on that Thanksgiving, but having passed the day in silence strongly connected to my soul, I felt a deeper tie to my inner self and to those I love.

LAST WORDS

Simple Gifts

Songs of Encouragement

Called to Be A Healing Witness

Listening with Deep Presence

"Witness"

When I'm Discouraged

The Way It Is

Simple Gifts

Uncomplicated acts of encouragement surprise me.

The traditional Shaker song begins "'Tis a gift to be simple" and I always delight to hear Aaron Copeland's orchestral suite, "Appalachian Spring," which includes the tune.

This very week I received several simple gifts—moments of politeness and helpful generosity, of grace—each a surprise. Moments in the shoe store, during a medical phone call, and in the parking lot. These moments encouraged my spirit to carry on.

On Monday, Denny, the shoe salesman, found just the right footwear for my problematic feet, accommodating my brace and orthotics perfectly. Afterward, he walked me to the door. Not only had Denny's attention to my specialized needs encouraged me to believe I might get around more easily, but also his welcome touch of civility gave me a feeling of hope for continued personal assistance.

On Wednesday, Lori, the technician who helped administer my nuclear stress test, called. Having been alerted by my cardiologist that I should check the test results online, it surprised me when Lori called with the news that they'd found a small blockage. I hadn't expected that human touch. "I'm calling to reassure you, David," she said. "We will care for you. Please just go easy on yourself right now." Lori's affirmation encouraged the real possibility that I could, indeed, let go of unrealistic worry.

On Friday, a stranger came to my assistance in the hospital parking lot after my physical therapy session. When it was time to exit the building, rain was falling in torrents and I'd forgotten to take an umbrella with me. As I prepared to try to make some kind of run for it, this fellow, who could have been a lineman for the Green Bay Packers, suddenly came alongside me with his correspondingly gigantic umbrella. "Okay, my man, where's your car? I'll take you to it, this parasol is for the two of us." Once safely inside the car, I called out, "What's your name?" He called back, "Samuel is my name, and it's been a pleasure keeping you dry today. Take care, my man."

Simple, encouraging offerings. Walking me to the door. Calling me with a difficult finding and using caring, careful words. And, shepherding me across a rain-swept parking lot. Each, such a welcome, uncomplicated gift.

Songs of Encouragement

Over a lifetime, friends show up just when needed most.

A song sparrow calls our front yard his home. Perched on the telephone wire just above our garden gate, he sings his song from dawn to dusk. It's a jubilant sound, quite full-throated and clear. I find the sound reassuring, promising, and, especially, encouraging.

This song sparrow has become a significant contributor to my life. He is steadily present. He brings joyfulness to my doorstep. He urges me to listen. His calm and unruffled song invites me to remember. I'm inspired to recall the attributes and actions of friends who've similarly calmed, steadied, and encouraged me.

These friends are steadfast. They always show up. They're hopeful, regardless of whatever devastation or disappointment they've experienced in their own lives. They are "in spite of everything, yes" people.

I recollect three notable instances of my friends steadying and encouraging me.

My "all is well" friends have a knack for showing up at the perfect moment. When I'd just been released from intensive care after brain tumor surgery, Roland, who lived half a continent away, paid me an unexpected visit. He surprised me by walking into my new hospital room carrying two brightly colored lobster buoys, which he'd brought all the way from the sea just beyond his home in Maine. My comrade presented the buoys to me with these words of encouragement, "Just like lobster fishermen, we rely on each other to stay afloat." Yes, all his efforts, the colorful metaphor of the buoys, and his broad smile helped keep me afloat for days on end. I still have the buoys, more than thirty-five years and numerous moves later.

Another time, upon hearing that I'd lost my bid to become Commissioner of Education for the state of Alaska, Gary called, inviting me to meet him at a local coffee shop. As I sat down, I noticed he'd brought a poem for me to read. Its title caught my attention immediately: "To A Friend Whose Work Has Come to Triumph."

Gary proceeded to read Anne Sexton's verses to me. The lines that called out most boldly were:

...think of innocent Icarus who is doing quite well:

larger than a sail, over the fog and the blast

of the plushy ocean, he goes. Admire his wings!

On seeing my startled reaction, Gary added, "Here's the punch line, David: Who cares that he fell back to the sea?" Here were both Anne Sexton and my friend actually celebrating failed efforts. We talked about this ancient Greek story of the man, Icarus, who crafted wings of wax but flew too close to the sun and how it applied to my life. Gary then invited me to join him for a brisk, two-mile hike. I remember well Gary's gifts to me that day—the surprisingly uplifting poem and that refreshing walk when with each step, my posture improved, and my spirit soared higher.

Finally, as a new member of the faculty at Lewis & Clark College in Portland, Oregon, I was beginning my academic career again. I was missing the many friends I'd made in Alaska over the decade just passed. I was feeling a sense of loss. I wondered would I ever again experience the comforting yet challenging feeling of being part of a true community.

Fortunately, my concern did not last long. Beginning at the first faculty meeting, I felt welcomed when I was invited to become a member of the college's Core Curriculum Committee. There was one particular endeavor our group initiated that both grounded me in my new home and also gave me a renewed sense of community. We decided to write an article together. One meeting we began talking about activities in our lives that we valued and enjoyed and how they had become metaphors that described and shaped our teaching. As an example, Caryl wrote,

"Teaching is like the ocean in its vastness and ever-changing nature; I can never quite get my arms around it. I can't ever comprehend its complexity, its beauty, its meaning."

Our writing project resulted in some of the most joyful and thought-provoking workplace conversations any of us had experienced as college professors. The time I spent engrossed in dialogue with these new colleagues was both life giving and life changing. Each time we met, the words of Elizabeth O'Connor, an author I admired, came to mind for me: "A new work emerges that will help us to make green a desert place, as well as to scale another mountain in ourselves." Creative new work in community was at hand, and I was on a new adventure. After my retirement from teaching at the college, all five of my friends stayed close to me. Even now, Caryl remains a constant presence in my life.

Roland, who had helped me stay afloat; Gary, who had enhanced my spirit; and Caryl and my college companions, who had revived my sense of community, all filled my heart with abundant, expansive, and encouraging hope.

Just as hopefully, the song sparrow continues to give me his encouraging melodies. He's even closer to our front door today! His uplifting tune cannot be missed. His calm steadiness reminds me of times of constant presence I've felt from friends over a lifetime. My friends have been singing their unique, caring songs of hope and encouragement to me ever so lovingly. I've been blessed by their steady, unwavering support.

Called to Be a Healing Witness

A week with a wise theologian changes the way I listen.

For many years, I admired the work and writings of Henri Nouwen, the renowned Dutch Catholic priest, eminent theologian, and prolific writer. I was particularly fascinated by Henri's views on listening and healing. And so, in a moment of audaciousness, I wrote to Henri, who wouldn't have known me from Adam, and asked if I could arrange to have some time with him.

Henri surprised me with his immediate reply: "David, you are invited to be my guest at Daybreak, my L'Arche community home in Richmond Hill, Ontario. But you need to know you must be my house guest for an entire week, and you will be put to work."

A few weeks later, I was comfortably settled at Daybreak, just outside of Toronto. And, I was put to work; I passed my mornings and evenings assisting and supporting Frank, a core member of the community who, like most of his companions in this remarkable home, experienced significant developmental disabilities. Frank and I made shopping trips and played checkers together, and we attentively listened to one another. That was the way of life at Daybreak.

Every afternoon, Henri and I would meet in his study. Our time began with a prayer of gratitude that we offered together and then we would each have our turn talking and listening. Henri had specifically requested we come prepared with a question to ask the other. While he was very interested in, and listened intently to, my stories about my work in Alaska, as an example, he always closed our session by asking me, "How do you listen, David?" I did my best to explain how I tried listening for a person's passion and for the unique truth of their life. My explanations would always give rise to Henri's asking if I would like to hear about his "beliefs of the day." My eager response was always, "Yes, Henri, please share your thoughts with me."

One afternoon Henri said, "David, every one of us is called upon to be a healer. We need not be professional counselors to offer a listening ear. We can't be therapists, but we can be good friends. Every one of us yearns for a *proximus*, someone or a few some ones, who are genuinely close to us. We all crave someone who can be a witness to our truth, to our reality."

I returned to my work as a school leader, filled with inspiration from Henri and my experience at Daybreak. I tried to make the professional meetings I ran as conducive to listening as possible, for instance by inviting each person at the meeting to express a joy or concern as we began our time together. I encouraged teachers to make their parent-teacher conferences safe conversation spaces. Rather than teachers merely reporting about a child, with the parent doing all the listening in a one-sided encounter, teachers worked on asking open questions to elicit the parents' intimate understanding of their child. Teachers were then to listen deeply to the parents' perspective. In the university classes I taught for school leaders, I asked participants Henri's question, "How do you listen?"

My time as a school leader has ended, but Henri's influence has not. These days, with my friends and family, I try to first listen, refraining from adding my perspective just to get my two-cents in. In conversation, I try to ask an open and honest question, rather than leading someone in my predetermined direction. I try to watch their expressions directly instead of gazing away.

On my leaving Daybreak, Henri gave me a promise. "Remember, David, as listeners, we are healing witnesses with a quiet task: With a compassionate heart, we are to receive the stories of whoever crosses our path. If we do so, the world will be changed for the better. That's a promise."

For me, listening to others' stories with a compassionate

heart is an act of encouragement. And, in Henri's listening to me and offering his promise, I found encouragement for my own desire and effort to be a healing witness in the world.

Listening with Deep Presence

"Free" listening lets go of expectations.

I've always admired my son-in-law, Mark, a hospice chaplain. In his spare time, he positions himself on a street corner or at the farmer's market and holds up a sign that announces "Free Listening." And the people come. They share stories. Mark listens. Mark's listening encourages them and reinforces the value of listening in me.

Careful listening was at the heart of my work as an elementary school principal. I sought out conversations with each child, teacher, parent, and community member to learn what they considered important and significant in their lives. Often, they would share details about what brought them the most happiness. I'd listen and then I'd try to encourage them in what brought joy and satisfaction.

These days, in my elder years, my listening continues, as do my efforts at encouraging. But something has changed. In the past, I think I used listening as a skill or strategy or a way to build relationship. There was nothing wrong with that and many times, doing so was quite positive. Now that I tend to be less interested in listening to encourage an outcome, I notice that people seek me out as a listener more frequently and the people who do so are sometimes surprising. I'll be out on a stroll in the neighborhood and a fellow walker will turn to me and just start telling me about a life challenge that is bringing him pain. I arrive in a doctor's office and the physician I know well but only see once a year asks, "Before we begin, could I tell you about a problem that's arisen in my family?" The postal carrier hails me from across the street with "Wait, David, I need to get your take on a routing modification that will affect me beginning next week."

What's going on? I'm not carrying my son-in-law's "Free Listening" sign. I'm simply going about my life.

Perhaps people feel comfortable in my presence. Could it be that the news on the street, so to speak, is that I am a person who is at home with himself? Perhaps to others, I seem like a person who is "the real deal." Maybe, I'm seen as someone who listens with my heart and soul to another's heart and soul. (I certainly hope at least one of these perceptions is true to who I am.)

Here's a more fully developed guess: People on and off the street will not share important stories with just anyone. They will not approach someone who is agitated or upset. Rather, their heartfelt feelings and concerns are most readily shared with folks who show a sense of quiet and ease. They appreciate others who offer their listening with calm and care. I do not hold myself up as any special example, yet I have tried more recently to develop such quiet and calm and also, I have been given an increasing inner calm as a gift—that is, I've been graced.

For me—and I believe, for all of us—an inner place of calm is our true center. It is from this space that I can best listen. Maybe, my calmness and listening are simply more accessible to others because I am an elder. Possibly, deep listening without expectation helps others to touch their own sense of inner calm. That is, having another person listen with quiet, non-agitated presence might help someone stop, become more still and experience a moment of calm in themselves in the midst of their busy, often frenetic life.

I'm grateful for those who arrive for my calm listening. They, in turn, offer me their trust. I cherish their trust. I honor their trust. I find that because of the trust they've given me, I check my words with utmost care. Before responding, I ask myself: Is what I have to say tightly connected to what I've just heard? Or, does what I have to offer come from my selfish, crafted cleverness? Are the words I'm about to share coming from my soul, from that deeply calm and present center space in me? Are the words moving like a river lovingly within me? Are they from a place of grace? How may I be encouraging? I might respond with an observation or question meant to help them connect and listen to their own calm center.

These days, in the autumn time of my life, as I approach my 85th birthday, I'm at a pretty joyful, soulful, genuine place in myself. I don't have any particular expertise to pass along to others. I have no sophisticated schemes or strategies to offer those who pass my way. What I do have to offer others, however, is my simple, easy-going self, my unassuming presence.

I can sit with a person who is suffering. I can offer my quiet company. I can listen carefully. I can bear witness to the everyday joys and sorrows of family, friends, neighbors, or whoever stops me in my tracks. I can just be with another, and another, and another. I can offer my simple gift. I can just be, listening with my whole self, my presence.

Witness

Standing watch
With her, with him
Keeping the vigil,
Listening carefully.

Remaining steadfast
Deliberately waiting
Cherishing the quiet
Embracing silence

Resting together
One being heard
The other, a witness
To truth, to what's real.

—David Hagstrom

When I'm Discouraged

A five-stage process helps me when I'm down in the dumps.

When I am in pain or have received unsettling news, I move through five stages to get back to my customary equilibrium and stability. Over the years I've come to call these phases: *curl up, turn on the music, get out there, show up, and breathe in silence.* Moving through these stages helps to transform the discouragement I'm feeling about my personal situation.

I notice when something disconcerting or disheartening happens to me, I turn toward discouragement. Rather, when something difficult happens to someone else, particularly someone I care deeply about, my emotion turns more toward sadness and I move more immediately toward action.

Initially, on becoming aware that I'm not my characteristically optimistic self, I'm inclined to, in a metaphoric sense, curl myself into a ball and sulk in the corner of the room. Fortunately, most of the time that interlude is relatively short-lived. However, there are occasions when that interval converts to the belief that I'm frozen and stuck.

Thinking back over the past couple of years, I can recall three instances of *curling up* that lasted anywhere from thirty minutes to three days. These examples aren't the only ones, but they are vivid for me.

At the peak of a record winter-long snow barrage, our small, but (to me) perfect, greenhouse crashed to the ground. There were small bits of glass scattered an inch deep covering the floor and all of the planting trays. I felt devastated. My first reaction was: all is lost, it's impossible to rebuild. At the time, I was full of "woe is me." However, I found myself picking up the phone to call the owner of the company from which I'd purchased the greenhouse kit and after the winter finally passed, I began to rebuild the greenhouse.

Informed criticism about my writing can also bring me discouragement. When I've sent essays to friends or to an editor, I've done so believing that I've passed along my best work and the piece was pretty well completed. Then, having received what seemed like negative feedback, I've felt—if I'm honest— misunderstood. It's hard to accept that my work is lacking in clarity or examples. In such situations, my first reaction can be "forget it, Charlie." I don't want to throw out my piece, but I want to throw it in a corner. And, I want to sulk. Happily for everyone, I'm getting better about all this. I'm learning that it's my words that aren't understandable or are unclear, rather than it being a personal rebuff. My friends and my editor want to help me to help others understand my story and its meaning.

A final example of feeling like *curling up* came just recently. After I planned a fantastic trip to visit with good friends in Santa Fe, New Mexico, a health emergency took me to the hospital the day before our departure, and out of necessity and caution, my wife and I canceled our travel. I was extraordinarily disappointed, although grateful to have received the medical assistance I needed at the time. Once again, my first response, after getting over the scare, turned to "woe is me." For a while I *curled up* and felt thoroughly disheartened.

Thankfully, episodes of discouragement are rather few and far between in my life. Typically, at times of imbalance and uncertainty, coming as they do when I've received or noticed a discouragement, I eventually *turn on the music*.

Listening to what for me is uplifting music initially acts as a calming distraction from my situation. In fact, the mere act of *turning on the music* signals to me that "this too will pass" and alerts me that I'm on my way out of my discouragement. I'm reminded that I don't have to be stuck and the particular music tells me there's another way to see the world. I've created a playlist of twelve tunes, a set I call "Rebalancing David." My favorites are: "Oh, What A Beautiful Morning" from the 1942

Broadway musical; the Israel Kamakawiwo'ole version of the classic "Somewhere Over The Rainbow;" "This Little Light of Mine," sung by Fontella Bass; Willie Nelson's "On The Road Again;" and the Kris Delmhorst song, "Everything is Music." I like the thought passed along by Hans Christian Anderson that "Where words fail, music speaks." When I *turn on the music,* I do pay attention to the lyrics; however, it's the beat and the melody that truly enliven me.

My *turn on the music* experience usually leads to the third and more active stage of my re-balancing. I instinctively *get out there* among people. Over my lifetime, I've learned that the most important gift we can give others is our presence. If I could snap my fingers and have my spouse or a trusted friend appear to be with me, that person's presence might be enough to get me out of myself. Having one of them simply be with me would be much more consequential than receiving their guidance, advice, or consolation. But getting someone to come be with me is not always possible and sometimes I may need to *get out there* in a literal sense. Sometimes just going into the front yard, watching folks come by on their bicycles or on their walks feels therapeutic and, better yet, someone passing by may stop to say hello. A further step beyond is to go to the feed store or the bird shop, where someone talks with me about the things that I care about. I find myself feeling encouraged when I just *get out there.*

By the time I've arrived at *the get out there* stage of regaining my equilibrium, I'm also realizing the importance of simply *showing up* at those times that I'm tempted to retreat or withdraw. Because long-distance running is a favorite athletic pursuit among members of my family, I've long been fascinated by the stories of marathon competitors. One of my favorite contenders is Desiree "Des" Linden. Des Linden came in first place among women in the 2018 Boston Marathon. She was the first woman from the United States to win the marathon in thirty-three years. When interviewed at the finish line, she admitted there were so many times she just didn't want to get out there and run in Michigan's snow and cold. Instead, she told herself, "It's critical that I just show up. No matter what,

I *must show up*. Day after day, I must show up." I also know the necessity and value of this practice.

Having moved through *the curl up, turn on the music, get out there*, and *show up* phases that shift me out of discouragement, I've become quiet and calm. I'm ready to return to my simple and natural-feeling meditation practice. First thing in the morning, I roll out my yoga mat, set my timer for twenty minutes, put on my eyeshade, and position myself lying face-up on our living room floor. I simply focus on my breathing. Deep breath in. Deep breath out. Often, about halfway through my time, I find that I am inviting joyfulness into my life on my in-breath, and on the breath out, I am dismissing doubt and uncertainty from my life. I'm always surprised when the timer announces the conclusion of my meditation practice. And, I'm always quite content.

These are the readjustment phases that work for me. This is my way of recovery. I have found, over the years, that this is how I make the gradual transformation from discouragement to encouragement within myself. The adjustment does not occur overnight; for me it takes going through all of the necessary phases, sometimes cycles of them. Eventually, encouragement can be seen on the horizon. Another storm has passed.

The Way It Is

Encouraging is my way of being.

Here's a poem that's long been my favorite:

The Way It Is

There's a thread you follow. It goes among
things that change. But it doesn't change.
People wonder about what you are pursuing.
You have to explain about the thread.
But it is hard for others to see.
While you hold it you can't get lost.
Tragedies happen; people get hurt
or die; and you suffer and get old.
Nothing you do can stop time's unfolding.
You don't ever let go of the thread.

—William Stafford

As I've looked at my life, I see that my thread is "encouraging."
This thread earnestly reaches out from within me without much
conscious effort, from who I am in my truest self. We all have
a thread we follow, a way of being that reflects and expresses
our deepest nature. Encouraging is mine. At the same time,
I've had to work at refining my attitudes and actions related to
encouraging so that my motivations and manners are all about
the other person not about myself. Furthermore, my capacities
to encourage have been profoundly influenced by others who
have encouraged me over so many years. I've learned from those

who've encouraged me about how to encourage others. Finally, I deeply believe all of us can be encouragers; we don't have to be "born" with that gift.

I held tight to my "encouraging" thread during my sixty years as an educator. Beginning with my time as a high school teacher, I wanted to consistently support young people and adults to understand their aptitudes and talents; I wanted them to know their gifts and use them boldly, imaginatively, and creatively. I felt that the way I could best encourage them was to be an attentive presence in their lives, a good listener, and a constant cheerleader. As I look back, I can see that my intentions and efforts continued in the same vein as an elementary principal and school district leader, working to similarly cheer on children, teachers, and families. When I worked as a university professor, I tried to assist school leaders to identify their gifts and to use them in the best service of others. Over the years, and for each person I worked with in the educational system, I wanted to be their witness and encourager, as they recognized and lived out their passions, their talents, and their skills.

I also tried to encourage my children to be true to themselves as they were growing up. I remember clearly when my daughter, Susan, had been admitted to Grinnell College, from which I'd graduated, as well as to St. Olaf College. During her prospective student visit to St. Olaf, she'd fallen in love with the school. Sitting with the decision about which college to attend, tears streamed down her face.

"What's wrong?" I asked.

"I don't want to go to Grinnell," she murmured.

"Where do you want to go?"

"St. Olaf!" she quickly replied.

Then together we fell into what we now call The Susan Test, "Would you cry if you didn't go to Grinnell? Would you cry if you didn't go to St. Olaf?" Even in present times my wife and I use a version of The Susan Test to check in with each other about important decisions. And, now these days, my daughter encourages me. When I doubt my writing, she continues to tell me, "Dad, you're a storyteller and have been doing so all your life!" Aren't I so very fortunate to have such a relationship with my daughter?

My son, Bruce, began running during his elementary school years. All through the summers on our family farm, he'd race ahead of our beat-up truck when we drove visitors over the rutted drive to show them the view from the top of the ninety-two-acre property, where Bruce had built a fort. When he was about 12, I decided to join him running our city neighborhood as a way to both encourage Bruce and to further strengthen our relationship. My favorite photo of Bruce shows him when he is just beginning his avocation as a marathon runner. There I am in the picture running behind him, aiding and abiding as a companion. Now he says of me on Facebook and to my face, "My dad has always had my back; he's been my advocate. We're friends forever. He's always been there for me, come what may." We agree that we are Pals Forever. Aren't I so very fortunate to have such a relationship with my son?

These days, my disposition to encourage, especially with efforts at attentive listening and caring questions and responses, remains strong in me. But how am I to hold on to my thread now in my octogenarian years and possibly beyond?

David Whyte provides a clue, with his phrase, the "eldership of love" from *The Heart Aroused*, referring to "belonging in a deeper way to those people and things we have learned to love." In these elder years, I am ever more deeply belonging to and focused on my family, close-in friends who are like extended family, and paradoxically, folks I don't know intimately, such as those I meet in medical facilities, in shops, and on the street, as I walk my everyday path of life. As I encourage them in my personal "eldership of love," I belong more tightly and profoundly to them. And, they to me, even if only for a few brief moments.

Put simply, and at its best, encouragement is an act of love. It's been that all along, but now I see love more clearly as the true taproot of encouragement. If I love, I can encourage.

The time for me to encourage and love remains unknown yet it continues to unfold. I won't ever let go of the thread.

CLOSING WITH AN INVITATION

Thanks for reading my stories. The sharing of stories is a gift that's mine to give. I've always believed my roles in life are that of caring listener, observant witness, thoughtful encourager, and lively storyteller. I am not inclined toward preaching or explaining. As my high school English teacher told us, "If you tell me, it's an essay. If you show me, it's a story."

Of course, as a storyteller who is also a writer, I'd rather show than tell you. In the process, I hope to embody what Barry Lopez, one of America's premier essayists and short-story writers, has said about stories and the storyteller: "The storyteller is the person who creates an atmosphere in which wisdom reveals itself." For me, the storyteller, the story itself, and the listener or reader co-create that space in which wisdom might make itself known.

Given this viewpoint, as each day of my remembering, recording, and revising moves toward twilight, my wish is that you and I could join together in a storytelling circle. I'd share my stories of encouragement with you and you'd share your stories with me. Perhaps we'd sit around a campfire. As we listened to each other, we'd hear the life-giving truth that experiences of encouragement can provide us.

So, to my invitation:

You're Invited

First, I invite you to remember a time when someone encouraged you. Or, you might recall some meaningful situation, place, or experience that heartened or reassured you. Alternatively, maybe you've witnessed an act of encouragement. Who or what has been a "messenger of encouragement" in your life?

Tell yourself a story about that person, situation, time, or place. Let your imagination bring forth the details of the episode, such as who was involved, when it happened, the circumstances and scene, the way things played out, and what was said (or not).

Then, ask yourself what that episode of encouragement meant to you and your life. You may even want to write down this story and its meaning for you.

And then—here's the punch line—I encourage you to share your story and its meaning for you, either directly with the person who encouraged you or with someone or some organization who might want to know it. Set up a conversation or send a message or letter. If you are considering "going public" in *any* way, I urge you to check in for permission from anyone involved. Finally, some of you may want or need to do your sharing simply within your active imagination.

You might find, as I have, that sharing your experience of encouragement with a friend or family member is a gratifying experience. And, if the story can be shared with your encourager, both of you might be appreciative. Having received another's encouragement, telling and sharing your story can encourage others.

Now it's time for me to say my farewell. As you know from reading, I'm an old guy in my mid-eighties. For me, this is a time of grace and gratefulness. I've appreciated the countless opportunities that have come my way over a lifetime. Some have been life-giving from the start. Others were difficult, challenging, and ongoing. But it didn't matter whether the given situation was trouble-free or problematic, encouragement always played a constructive role.

As I look around, I notice the world doesn't need any more faultfinders. Having fine-tuned my watchfulness, I observe that almost everyone responds positively to thoughtful encouraging.

As for myself, even the simplest ways of encouraging invite me to be at ease. When I walk my neighborhood, a wave of the hand or someone tipping their cap brings a smile to my face. Words aren't necessary. Such recognition and kindness itself provides encouragement and so, hope.

Throughout my life, having received encouragement now inspires me to call out: Because of everything, yes!

May you be well. May you be at ease.

AFTERWORD: THEY CALLED OUT TO US

For more than a year, my wife, Karen, and I have been "sheltered in place," in Portland, Oregon. We've been most fortunate and privileged to reside in our own safe home during this COVID-19 pandemic, with resources we can afford. Still, it's been a challenging time, as it's been for so many, with its ongoing uncertainties. Yet, we've received gifts of support that beg for recognition and an expression of gratitude. I'm eager to share this encouraging story with you. But first, a few words about how we've been experiencing this frightening and bewildering pandemic.

We're an older couple: Karen's in her seventies, and I'm in my eighties, both of us with what are called "underlying conditions," and so now we are designated as "the most vulnerable." We are homebound, but luckily not due to ill health. And we are working hard to keep ourselves healthy! We're aware of our susceptibility; we carefully follow all of Oregon's directives. Our groceries are delivered. If we go for a walk, we obey the rules of social distancing and we wash our hands many times a day. Securing products to protect our health has taken time and creativity and, yes, we wash our hands after we handle those boxes that arrive at our doorstep.

During much of the past year we've found news reports to be conflicting, confusing, and chaotic. Searching high and low, we've often found a lack of empathy, grief support, or realistic encouragement from leadership at the national level. Something like Winston Churchill's wartime words would have been so appreciated and appropriate early in this time: "We have before us an ordeal of the most grievous kind. ... '[C]ome then, let us go forward together with our united strength.'"

We've tried our best to remain steady and stable with different days bringing a range of emotional states. Some days are peaceful; on another day one of us might feel agitated; a morning might feel joyful while the afternoon turns toward gloom. At times we wish we were more confident; feeling self-possessed is not always a first response. Without fail, however, we sit side-by-side for an hour each evening to read aloud from an inspirational book, look at photos of beautiful flowers from the day's neighborhood walk, share our experience of daily events, and sort out our feelings. Together, we are seeking to live with abiding hope that not only "all *is* well," but also that "all *will* be well."

❧◉◉☙

In the midst of our pandemic experience, we have, however, received encouraging measures of good cheer. Two improbable emissaries arrived at our front gate. It's not that these two folks have been unknown to us; we've known Anthony and Meghan for some time. We like them a lot! It's just that in this time, each has brought us gifts of unforeseen re-assurance and hope.

Anthony has served us well as our postal carrier for many years. He always waves his greeting with a smile as he passes by our home. We think the USPS can be proud of his work. Still, we were astonished when he leaned across our gate and exclaimed, "Anything that you folks need during these difficult times, I'll get for you." We were so surprised, we just called back, "Thank you, Anthony." Over these past months we've not asked him to retrieve items from the grocery store or pharmacy, although we have no doubt that he would have shopped for us before or after his postal service hours.

However, given our reluctance in these times to go into public spaces such as our local post office, we've asked for his assistance with postal tasks. For example, he's taken our packages and certified mail, keeping at the recommended social distance or more and, our having provided the necessary funds, he's attached the correct postage when he arrives back at the post office. He's kept us going during the pandemic. Anthony's pledge and reliability have made a tremendous difference in terms of our being able to accomplish basic tasks without increased risk, while also increasing our assurance that help will be provided. Moreover, we were both astonished and delighted when one day as he waved good-bye to us from across the street, he called out "Love you guys!" Without a doubt, we're grateful that Anthony is a messenger of encouragement.

These past couple of years, Meghan has come periodically to help us with yard and garden tasks that we can no longer handle on our own. She assists with weeding, lawn mowing, tree trimming, repairing our fence, and feeding the birds. She goes willingly beyond the "mow and go" of many lawn maintenance companies, for instance, by shoring up the wobbly steps in the backyard and the lopsided garden gate. She is conscientious and hardworking; her presence and dependability are making it possible for us to age in place, for which we feel deep appreciation. She helps us carry on.

Still, we were somewhat startled to hear Meghan call out to us on one visit early in the pandemic, and then repeatedly, "Whatever you need during this difficult time, I'll provide it for you. Just ask." We've made only one request of that sort from the grocery store, but knowing that we can count on her brings us important peace of mind and practical support should we need it.

We count on her attending to our garden and we're grateful that she, like Anthony, is willing and available to help us stay safe during this time of risks to our health. However, as time passes, we're realizing she tends our hearts as well. On the occasion of my 85th birthday, Meghan shared these words with me: "Thank you, David, for honoring me with your trust, and for permitting me to help tend your...garden. The kindness, interest, respect and care you have shown for me imbues my work with great value and meaning. Happy Birthday!" Meghan has been, for me and for us, another messenger of encouragement, for which we're immensely grateful.

In a time when everyday foundations have been shaken, two new friends have called out to us. And they have found their place right in the very center of our hearts.

Each morning, I read the words from a writer who inspires and encourages me. This morning, I've been reading the words of Thomas Merton, the American Trappist monk and prolific writer, from a lecture entitled "True Freedom" that he gave to novices at the Abbey of Gethsemani in Kentucky, just prior to his death.

In this lecture, Merton speaks to what he believes remains of us once we die: "The little kernel of gold that is the essence of you." Although I'd encountered this general idea before, I was gripped by Merton's characterization and his additional language of "this little grain of gold," which I take to refer to the very unchanging center of each of us.

Although I'm likely skimming the surface of Merton's insight, at the time of my reading I was reminded that there is more to each of us than what we see on the surface. I believe Anthony and Meghan have given us a glimpse into the essence of each of them, their true selves, who they are at their very core.

Finally, I'm reminded of the words of Albert Camus, the French novelist and playwright: "In the midst of winter, I've found an invincible summer." In the midst of this tragic, life-threatening, destructive pandemic, we've been given lifelines. In the midst of an ominous storm, Meghan and Anthony called out to us. They noticed us. They have encouraged us profoundly.

You Reading This, Be Ready

Starting here, what do you want to remember?
How sunlight creeps along a shining floor?
What scent of old wood hovers, what softened
sound from outside fills the air?

Will you ever bring a better gift for the world
than the breathing respect that you carry
wherever you go right now? Are you waiting
for time to show you some better thoughts?

When you turn around, starting here, lift this
new glimpse that you found; carry into evening
all that you want from this day. This interval you spent
reading or hearing this, keep it for life –

What can anyone give you greater than now,
starting here, right in this room, when you turn around?

—William Stafford

GRATITUDES

Sharing these stories gives me the opportunity to express my gratitude. I've been so fortunate over my lifetime. Family members, friends, neighbors, and even complete strangers have encouraged me and this book. I appreciate each and every act of recognition and inspiration, every act that gave me heart and quiet courage.

I don't think I'd have been able to write this book without the people, places, and opportunities that have especially encouraged and energized my writing practice over time and at critical points, which I list here chronologically, starting with the earliest: the Green Lake (WI) Writing Conference offered my very first taste of being in the company of other writers in a workshop setting; Roland Barth and my friends at the Harvard Principals' Center called out my written reflections about school leadership; William Demmert, while Commissioner of Education for the State of Alaska, opened my eyes to Alaska Native ways of knowing and invited me into written dialogue about Alaska Native education; Carolyn Servid and the Island Institute in Sitka, Alaska, gave me the opportunity to be in conversation with renown writers, such as the poet William Stafford; the Northwest Writing Institute at Lewis & Clark College, Kim Stafford, Director, as well as the Core Committee of L & C's Graduate School of Education, prompted my writing about teaching in higher education; Michael Glaser at St. Mary's College of Maryland arranged a sojourn for me as an artist-in-residence; sabbatical time in France provided space, inspiration and writing desks that greeted me each morning at the Provençal farmhouse and in Alexandra's Paris apartment; the Northwest Narrative Medicine Collaborative encouraged me to delve more deeply into my personal medical experiences and as a patient in the health care system; Marcy Jackson has always been there to share meaningful conversation and just the right resource to fit my needs and interests; and across so many years, another long-time friend, Courage & Renewal co-facilitator, and writing colleague, Caryl Casbon, has always offered her thoughtful listening and creative perspective. And, without fail, the Writing House itself.

Although it would be quite unlikely that he would see himself in this way, I consider Parker J. Palmer to be a mentor for me. I do not have the right words to describe how influential he has been to who I am as a person and to my work in the world. I am so very grateful for his belief in me and his support of this book by writing its Foreword.

Others have also shown their belief in this book during its time of preparation. My at-a-distance editors, Michele Regenold and Megan LeBoutillier, have clarified the traces of my ideas, de-mystified cluttered stories and helped keep me on the straight and narrow with all the rules of grammar. I have also been particularly inspired by Michele's transparency and personal tenacity in her own trying times. My at-home editor, Karen, through her thought-provoking questioning, imaginative sense of finding the best way forward, and language has transformed the manuscript. Karen is the love of my life, and so, with gratitude, I dedicate this book to her. I also greatly appreciate Kim Cooper Findling, publisher of Dancing Moon Press, and her team who have all carefully shepherded this book through its publishing process.

Finally, I offer my thanks to all the readers of my words across the years and now, here in this book. Your doing so has helped me believe in myself.

I give these stories to my family and friends. Please accept this gift as an expression of my gratitude. Over the years, I have cherished you and now, I cherish you even more. Thank you for believing in me.

In my favorite book, *Jayber Crow*, Wendell Berry writes about the mythical community of Port William, Kentucky, describing people in the town in this way: "...I saw them all as somehow perfected, beyond time, by one another's love, compassion, and forgiveness, as it is said we may be perfected by grace." I wrote the stories in this book in the spirit of gratitude for all those who have encouraged and loved me into my best self and for the ways that I've been, if not perfected, then changed for the better, certainly by others, and undoubtedly by grace.

Encouragement is something we can all offer each other. It does not have to be complicated and can even be seen and experienced as a close cousin of kindness. Most of us respond agreeably to offers of kindness and encouragement. Many of us feel more seen, understood and resilient as a result of such simple acts. May we all be somehow perfected by another's encouragement. With encouragement, may we all contribute to a more kind-spirited and compassionate world, one person at a time.

RESOURCES

Sources of Earlier Versions of Individual Stories

Earlier versions of "The Truth-Telling Hour" and "The Ice Rink Lesson" were published in the *Grinnell College Magazine.*

Earlier versions of "The Ice Rink Lesson," "Getting Out of My Brain," and "Walking Them Home" were published in *From Outrageous To Inspired: How To Build a Community of Leaders in Our Schools* by David Hagstrom (2003/2004). San Francisco: Jossey-Bass Publishers (ISBN 0-7879-7066-2).

Notes

In "Welcome," the quotation beginning "My story is not important because...." is to be found in *Telling Secrets* (p. 30) by Frederick Buechner. New York, NY: Harper Collins (1991).

In "Welcome," the quotation stating "I have only what I remember" is to be found in the poem "A Likeness" in *The Shadow of Sirius* by W. S. Merwin. Port Townshend, WA: Copper Canyon (2008).

The poem "Greatest Gift" is to be found in *Making Contact* by Virginia Satir. Millbrae, CA: Celestial Arts (1976).

In the section "Vocation's Early Days," the quotation by Rumi that begins "When you do things..." is to be found at https://www.goodreads.com/quotes/32894-when-you-do-things-from-your-soul-you-feel-a.

In the section "The Wisconsin Farm," the quotation by Celeste Holm that begins "We live by encouragement..." is to be found at https://www.goodreads.com/quotes/1065510-we-live-by-encouragement-and-die-without-it--slowly.

In the section "Medical Encounters," the poem "The Quiet Place" is a previously unpublished one by David Hagstrom.

In the story "Honor the People," the poem excerpt is from the unpublished "Honor the People; It's the Leader's Work" by David Hagstrom (copyrighted 2004).

In the section "Alaskan Treasures," the poem "Gentle Man, Be with Us" is a previously unpublished one by David Hagstrom.

In the section "The Gifts of Travel," the quotation by Ibn Battuta beginning "Traveling..." is to be found at https://www.goodreads.com/quotes/508820-traveling-it-leaves-you-speechless-then-turns-you-into-a.

In the story "Songs of Encouragement," the quotation beginning "think of innocent Icarus..." is to be found in the poem, "To A Friend Whose Work Has Come to Triumph" in *The Complete Poems: Anne Sexton* by Anne Sexton. New York, NY: Mariner Books (1999).

In the story "Songs of Encouragement," the article written with my Lewis & Clark College colleagues ("Teaching Is Like...?") was published in *Educational Leadership*, Volume 57, No. 8, May 2000 (pp. 24-27).

In the story "Songs of Encouragement," the quotation beginning "A new work emerges..." by Elizabeth O'Connor can be found at https://friendsofsilence.net/quote/source/cry-hope.

In the section "Last Words," the poem "Witness" is a previously unpublished one by David Hagstrom.

In the story "The Way It Is," the poem "The Way It Is" is to be found in *Ask Me: 100 Essential Poems* by William Stafford and the Estate of William Stafford. Minneapolis, MN: Graywolf Press (1977, 1980, 1998).

In the story "The Way It Is," the quotation beginning "belonging in a deeper way..." is to be found in *The Heart Aroused: Poetry and the Preservation of the Soul in Corporate America* (p. 210) by David Whyte. New York, NY: Currency Doubleday (1994).

The poem "You Reading This, Be Ready" is to be found in *Ask Me: 100 Essential Poems* by William Stafford and the Estate of William Stafford. Minneapolis, MN. Graywolf Press (1977, 1980, 1998).

In "Closing With An Invitation," the quotation beginning, "the person who creates..." is a statement by Barry Lopez, which is to be found on the wall of the entrance to the Deschutes County Library in Bend, Oregon. It is reportedly taken from Barry Lopez's description of the role of the writer, which can be located at https://lannan.org/bios/barry-lopez.

In the "Afterword," the quotation that begins "We have before us..." by Winston Churchill is to be found at https://winstonchurchill.org/resources/speeches/1940-the-finest-hour/blood-toil-tears-and-sweat-2/.

In the "Afterword," the reference to "this little kernel of gold" and "this little grain of gold" are to be found in the lecture entitled "True Freedom" by Thomas Merton, transcribed by Cynthia Bourgeault for the cassette series "Sufism: Longing for God." Kansas City: Credence Cassettes (1995).

In the "Afterword," the well-known quotation from Albert Camus is to be found at https://www.goodreads.com/quotes/508603-in-the-midst-of-winter-i-found-there-was-within.

In the "Gratitudes," the quotation beginning "I saw them all as somehow perfected..." is to be found in *Jayber Crow* (p. 205) by Wendell Berry. New York, NY: Counterpoint LLC (2000.)

About the Author

David Hagstrom is a storyteller and writer, educator and community builder. He received his formal education at Grinnell College, Harvard University, and the University of Illinois. With this foundation, David served as a teacher, school leader and university professor in the Midwest, Alaska and Oregon for over 50 years. He has facilitated retreats in the Pacific Northwest and nationally based on the work of Parker J. Palmer through the Center for Courage & Renewal. Periods of immersion in Alaska, Hawaii, Sweden (his family's homeland), France, Spain, Japan and South Korea also formed his personhood and perspective. In all these settings, David experienced and learned about the life-changing impact of genuinely encouraging words and actions.

Over his lifetime, David has felt and expressed a love of the land. He has always enjoyed working in the dirt, tending seeds and plants, and became a Master Gardener while living in Alaska. David especially cherishes his nickname "Farmer Dave." These days, his favorite place to do "dirt work" is on land north of Sisters, Oregon, which is lovingly christened The Clearing.

His wife, Karen, and his adult children, Susan and Bruce, are his greatest encouragers.

David can be contacted at davidalanhagstrom@yahoo.com.

The photo at left, bottom, is David's treasured Writing House, which sits at The Clearing in Central Oregon.

"David Hagstrom has been a messenger of encouragement in my life for many years, and now I have the good luck to possess his wisdom, compassion, and buoyant companionship in the storm of life by reading this book. Years ago, when David was working to support teachers and school administrators, he told me "I start in November, when the dark weather comes. That's when people need to get together and help each other." This impressed me as unusually insightful—David's instinct to bring help to the exact time and place it's needed. In this book, you will find and come to treasure many such encounters. You will learn the origin stories of David's legendary gift for connecting, asking, and listening. This book will guide your own recognition of the people who have helped you, and will shape new ways for you to help others in these mysterious times."

—Kim Stafford, Oregon's Ninth Poet Laureate and Founding Director, Northwest Writing Institute

"In our noisy world, it is a delight to slow down and be nourished by the wisdom in David's stories. Each one serves as a reminder of the various ways we can be present to each other—observing, listening carefully, and acting in ways that support another's flourishing. David's memoir is a testament to the true role of a witness and the quiet but essential work of encouragement that is always necessary, but desperately required in today's complex world."

—Chris M. Murchison, Positive Organization Advocate and Coach

"With these simple and elegant stories, each a window into his own long life, David Hagstrom invites us to view our own lives as a series of "encouragements," gifts of love and kindness bestowed on us by others. From childhood teachers who saw in a quiet boy more promise than he found in himself, to nurses in the ICU who saved his life by salvaging his hope; from friends who've known him well enough to speak the truth in love, to strangers in unlikely times and places, the messengers we meet in these pages are plain-spoken, hard-working and wondrous. Hagstrom reminds us that good companions abound in our lives, if we take the time to notice, and that gratitude is best expressed when we pass the gift along, becoming messengers ourselves of life-giving, generous encouragement. To encourage means, literally, "give heart;" these stories are large-hearted, intimate glimpses of a grateful and attentive life."

—Victoria Safford, Lead Minister, White Bear Unitarian Universalist Church

Made in the USA
Middletown, DE
08 May 2021